Unknown Happiness

Klaudia Tran

Dedication

"To the beautiful souls worldwide, your light inspires this story. Thank you."

Contents

Chapter One
Beneath The Surface: Exploring The Complexities Of Early Life

In my life, I've passed through valleys that seemed bottomless, climbed peaks that touched the sky, and moved the unpredictable rhythm of fate. Today, as I pen down the story of my existence, it's not just a memoir; it's an outstretched hand to those who, like me, have stumbled in the dark, searching for the light.

Life, for me, has been a rollercoaster, a relentless journey through a complex pattern of experiences. The lows outnumbered the highs, but in the depths of despair, I unearthed resilience. I've faced toxic relationships, weathered storms within family and partnerships, and survived the chilling embrace of a gunshot. Yes, life has dealt me blows that would have shattered many, but it never extinguished the flame of hope within me.

This isn't a tale of victimhood; it's a testament to the extraordinary strength within ordinary lives. From a mentally abusive ex-husband to choices that led me astray, each ordeal, instead of becoming a stumbling block, became a stepping stone. Through the bruises, both visible and hidden, I learned. I evolved. And most importantly, I discovered an unshattered faith in the possibility of a good life.

As I share my experiences, I don't claim to have all the answers. I'm not a sage or a guru. I am you, and you are me—two souls entwined in the struggle for a life that echoes with happiness and love. This journey is not about the darkness I faced; it's about the light I discovered within that darkness. It's a call to everyone who has felt the weight of despair: believe. Believe that change is possible, that redemption is never out of reach, and that, no matter how late the hour, a good life is still within grasp.

This is my story. It's raw, imperfect, and, above all, a homage to the enduring power of the human spirit. So, let's embark on this journey together—a journey of hope, resilience, and the strong belief that, indeed, anything is possible.

Beginning from my childhood, a journey filled with stains of pain and yearning unfolds with memories that cling like shadows.

Within the contours of my past lies a shattering wave of pain with only a singular purpose—to offer solace to those who tread a path akin to mine. The genesis of my journey, cloaked in the haze of early childhood, is marked by a haunting absence of joy.

My earliest recollections flicker into view like distant stars. A poignant memory of three, a fragile yet vivid moment, involves a stroll with my grandmother. The hospital looms in the background, where my mother stands wrapped in a pink bathrobe, waving through a window—a tender memory in a landscape dominated by shadows.

However, at six, the darkness in my story deepened, the age when I started to develop the sense of understanding things and conscious mind. The father tirelessly immersed in providing, working relentlessly to stave off hunger and provide the semblance of a stable life. The mother, a teacher, with her focus fixated not on familial bonds but on societal perception—an external facade overshadowing the internal disturbance.

At home, a place that should have been a haven of warmth and nurturing instead transformed into a battleground. Weekends carried the heavy scent of alcohol, and amidst the haze, family ties started to lose. My mother, once a dedicated educator, became a skilled architect of this facade, constructing an illusion of virtue for the outside world while our internal world crumbled.

As the youngest, I was the most affected by all that chaos. Weekends were not spent in the soothing embrace of familial ties but in the company of adults—friends who, too, were trapped in the journey of intoxication. Forced to find a place on the floor to rest my head, the supposed sanctuary of home became a makeshift refuge with no sense of belonging.

Yet, amid the chaos, a beacon emerged—an idyllic escape by the lake. A house, a haven built by my father, where summer unfolded in a symphony of sunlit days and childhood laughter. Those two months served as a respite from the storm within, offering a fleeting taste of what could be construed as a happy childhood.

That lake, to me, stood as a symbol of the contradictions in my upbringing. While the chaos of our home life echoed within its waters, the lake transformed into a place to hide and a place where friendships bloomed.

Amid it all at home, the lake became our refuge, a place of solace and healing. It wasn't just a body of water; it was our escape from the cramped apartment and the emotional dysfunction within our family.

The lake held a special meaning for all of us. It wasn't just a place to swim; it was a place that provided a break from the struggles of our daily lives. The freedom to explore the outdoors and the calming effect of the water made it a haven, a stark contrast to the oppressive atmosphere at home.

Summers by the lake were a welcome respite. The warmth of the sun, the laughter of friends, and the simple joy of swimming created a world far removed from the challenges we faced. It became an annual tradition, a two-month reprieve from the usual difficulties, allowing my mother to relax and enjoy life without the burden of work.

The lake wasn't just a recreational spot; it was an anchor in the storm of our family dynamics. Cold weather, often associated with depression and heightened tensions, magnified the struggles within our apartment. Winters were marked by my mother's cold and sometimes harsh demeanor, a stark contrast to the warmth of the summers by the lake.

My dislike for cold weather, lingering into adulthood, stems from those challenging times. The warmth of summer, symbolized by the lake, represented safety and a temporary escape from the harsh realities of home.

The lake, with its friendly embrace and the laughter of childhood companions, was my haven. In the simplicity of play and the joy of swimming, I found respite from the complexities that haunted the walls of my home. It was here that I made a friend, and together, we passed every week, reveling in the freedom of youth and peace offered by the waters.

As I look back on the formative years of my existence, the memories unfold like ripples on the serene surface of the lake, revealing the hidden turbulence beneath. At the age of six, the echoes of my parents' arguments, fueled by the intoxicating effects of alcohol, painted a somber background of the drama that played out in a repetitive mode in our lakeside residence.

In a perpetual quest for external affirmation, my mother constantly sought attention from other men. Witnessing this as a child left a scarring mark on my young heart, stirring an unsettling discomfort within me.

My mom's habit of sitting on strangers' laps remained unchanged despite my pleas for her to stop. This peculiar scene unfolded amidst the bonfires and social gatherings at the lake house, creating a jarring contrast between the apparent joy of family gatherings and the internal discord threatening to break us.

A particularly poignant moment etched in my memory occurred during a heated argument between my parents. The conflict escalated to a physical confrontation, leaving my older siblings and me to grapple with the unsettling reality what our family, the supposed bedrock of love and support, was indulged in before our eyes. With significant age gaps between us, the three siblings witnessed a breakdown that defied the very essence of familial bonds.

This heart-wrenching incident also took place when I was only six. My mom and dad were hosting a party, and my mother overdosed, as usual, and came under the heavy influence of booze and lost control.

I can still recall that picture in front of my eyes: my mother hitting my dad, and my dad simply pushing her onto the ground and holding her there. He wasn't physically abusing her; rather, he was merely attempting to comfort her. But you don't realize that when you're a child.

Something similar happened to me, and I then ran to my uncle, who lived next door. He was feeling very summer house-y. And he was, I believe, with two prostitutes when I went there.

Two sex workers. Everybody was naked. Then, before I could even go to my uncle, he quickly changed into his clothes and followed me outside, where I screamed for aid. And he held on to my mom and just tried to calm the situation.

We then proceeded to the house thereafter, where he spent the night with us till my mom slept away, as she was prone to being combative after drinking. And she still is as of right now.

Our home was always in chaos, and my mother's emotional distance and self-destructive habits added to the darkness of the situation. She didn't just criticize; she subjected us to both emotional and physical abuse. Meals, instead of being a comforting routine, turned into battlegrounds, with portions dictated not by hunger but by my father's plate.

The narrative of my upbringing continues to circle back to my mother, a complex figure whose emotional well-being became a defining factor for my ruthless childhood. Her own upbringing, shaped by a household of twelve, cast shadows of toxicity that she, in turn, carried into her own family.

Born as the third child, my mother assumed the role of caretaker for her siblings in the face of her parents' challenges—an alcoholic father and an overwhelmed mother. Instead of breaking free from this toxic pattern, she unwittingly transplanted it into her own household, raising a cycle she had known intimately.

Weekends in our home were synonymous with a different kind of ritual—drinking. My mother sought attention not from my father but from anyone but him. It felt like there was an undercurrent of resentment towards him, yet a fear that kept her tethered to the relationship. Our living conditions mirrored the discord within our family—a small, prison-like apartment, a testament to our financial struggles.

The living arrangements were far from conventional. I shared a bedroom with my brothers, while my sister, who was eleven years older, occupied a room alone. Here, the echoes of my mother's own upbringing surfaced. In a twist of fate, she placed the responsibility of caring for me onto my sister, mirroring the burdens she had once shouldered for her own siblings.

The symmetry of this generational repetition became painfully clear. My sister, much like my mother in her youth, found herself burdened with the role of raising a younger sibling. It wasn't a fair expectation for a child to bear the responsibility of nurturing another. While occasional help and play were reasonable, the weight of raising a sibling should not have rested on her young shoulders.

The injustice of this situation laid bare the cyclical nature of dysfunction within our family. The very duty my mother had undertaken in her own childhood had now become a source of tension and resentment in our home. Our lives became stages where the challenges passed down through generations and unaddressed pain formed the threads. It created a picture of difficulties and lost chances for positive change.

Sleep, something that should have been a normal routine factor for a child, became tinged with fear. Shadows played tricks on my young mind, leading to a nightly ritual of calling out to my father for reassurance. The fear of the dark, a tangible manifestation of the unseen specters haunting my psyche, persisted as a haunting presence.

At six, a significant shift occurred—no longer allowed to sleep with my mother, I was thrust into the confined space of a room shared with my brothers. The loss of that intimate connection marked another chapter in a childhood defined by the absence—of love, support, and the emotional security every child craves.

These fragments from my past pieced together, paint a vivid picture of a complex childhood lacking the warmth and stability every child deserves. The scars of those formative years became the driving force behind my quest for healing and the foundation of the understanding I hoped to impart to others.

In the tangled web of my childhood, my mom was a mysterious figure struggling with her own demons. The tension between my parents was obvious, and looking back, I realize it wasn't just physical distance but an emotional disconnect. The cozy nights next to my dad were abandoned, casualties of a loveless marriage. It's a truth that's taken time to sink in, a puzzle piece falling into place as I revisit the early chapters of my life.

My mom's actions, once confusing, now seem like desperate bids to escape a joyless marriage. Seeking attention from other men became her way of coping, a sad attempt to find validation when real love was absent. I get it now; it's tough to share a bed with someone you don't love. The complexities of grown-up relationships, a mystery to me as a kid, now make sense.

Returning to the story of my childhood, memories of my mom are intertwined with moments that define my struggle for identity. She pushed me into a singing competition, thinking it would be good for me. Little did she know, her frustrated words would stick with me, turning the joy of singing into a hidden fear of judgment.

As I grew up, my dad, always physically there, remained a quiet figure. He became a dad at 40, unusual for those times, and our outings were tinged with awkward assumptions about our relationship. But underneath that discomfort was a good man. I remember going to the store with him, and someone mistaking him for my granddad. His correction was simple but meant everything.

Yet, expressing emotions remained a challenge. My dad, a pillar of strength, struggled to say, "I love you." His love language was quiet support and unspoken sacrifices that took me years to understand. And after seven decades of life, he finally said the words I needed to hear.

The intricate interchange of love and understanding in my family became a defining theme of my childhood. Mom chasing fleeting affirmations, dad offering silent support—it made for a complex emotional landscape. These factors shaped my upbringing—a story marked by insecurities, unspoken love, and a journey to find myself.

Growing up, the absence of my mother's affirmations left a profound mark. While other kids enjoyed the warmth of a mother's love, my experience was the opposite. The person who should have been my best friend, my confidante, was instead a source of mental abuse and constant belittlement.

As a child, you naturally look to your mother for love and support. It's an instinctive bond, an expectation of care and affection. However, my reality was starkly different. My mother never said, "I love you," or expressed pride in my achievements. The void left by this emotional neglect lingered, an unspoken burden that weighed heavily on my young shoulders.

The contrast became stark when I visited a friend's house after kindergarten. We were both innocent, dreaming of imaginary families, crafting scenarios of love and happiness. It was a poignant escape from the harsh reality of our lives. Her mother, divorced and seeking solace in our shared moments, showered us with praise for the simplest things.

Elementary school ushered in a new form of torment—I became a target of bullying. The reason was simple: I looked different. Weight gain became a catalyst for the cruelty of my peers. Meanwhile, my mother unwittingly added to the ridicule by dressing me in clothes meant for my sister, who was eleven years my senior.

Imagine trying to blend in when you're already struggling with obesity and wearing outdated clothes that attract even more ridicule. My mom's response was dismissive, claiming she wouldn't spend money on new clothes for me, insisting the old ones were sufficient.

When I tried to tell her about the bullying, she shifted the blame onto me, suggesting that I must be annoying the other kids. In her eyes, it was always my fault, and she offered little support. This made me feel incredibly lonely at school as I struggled to make friends in the face of constant judgment and ridicule.

The scars of those early years run deep, shaping my perception of self and family. The void left by my mother's emotional absence was palpable, a void that couldn't be filled by imaginary scenarios or the fleeting praise of a friend's parent. The quest for healing and understanding began, a difficult journey fueled by the desire to break free from the traps of a shaky past.

The absence of a supportive maternal figure intensified my sense of isolation. While other kids sought refuge in the warmth of their mothers, my pursuit of comfort was met with dismissal and condemnation. Seeds of self-doubt, planted in the fertile ground of my early years, took root, creating a narrative filled with the troubling web of insecurity.

As I walked through the corridors of my formative years, the contrast between what should have been my life and what was actually my life became starker. Childhood, a time meant for innocence and joy, was a battlefield where insecurities took root. And so, the journey continued, unraveling the layers of pain, seeking a path to self-discovery and healing

Chapter Two
Battleground Of Teenage Years: Struggles Amidst Chaos

The shadows of my distressing childhood loomed over my school years like an unshakeable storm cloud, relentless and unforgettable. The scars etched by emotional neglect and the never-ending chaos at my home seemed to seep into every phase of my school life as well, casting an unmatched shadow upon my teenage years.

Growing up in a household filled with constant yelling, depression, and fights was a battle on its own. My parents fought ceaselessly, and my mom's actions were no different, generating an environment devoid of love or care. It felt like everyone was on their own, left to navigate the chaos alone. Home was merely a place to sleep and eat, but emotionally, it was barren.

Depression, that constant, heavy companion, walked with me through the corridors, lurking behind every forced smile and every attempt to fit in. It wasn't just a memory; it was a relentless reality that clung to me, shaping my thoughts, my interactions, and my perception of the world around me.

The weight of those early years, the peer pressure, the neglect—they didn't just linger in the past. They followed me in the hallways of my middle school and echoed in my heart, a constant reminder that happiness was elusive, a factor I always yearned for but struggled to attain.

So, to begin with, in middle school, life became a battleground. Home became a dark place, devoid of the warmth and care a child craves. My parents' constant battles became the soundtrack to my existence, a constant reminder of the void that needed filling. That's when I sought solace in the wrong places, hoping to find peace where there was none.

I turned to smoking, finding comfort in cigarettes, a misguided attempt to discover happiness outside the shaken boundaries of home. It wasn't just about the cigarette smoke; it was a quest for acceptance and peace, elements absent in the place I should have found them most—my home.

The pain of being unwanted and unnoticed at home pushed me toward a desperate search for acceptance, and I lost control. The crowd I was sitting with started sharing their cigarettes and vodka, and I eagerly joined in, craving the sense of belonging I had long longed for.

Not to mention that I was only 14 when I went away with my friends and drank my first-ever vodka. Yeah! We were only four people, all 14, and we finished two bottles of vodka by ourselves.

This event was followed by an ill-fated Valentine's Day at school, when we drowned ourselves in alcohol, oblivious to the dangers. During the biting cold of that winter evening, we teenagers embarked on a misadventure fueled by recklessness and a thirst for acceptance. As we went from the freezing cold outside to the warm school, the more we drank, the crazier things got. It was like everything went out of control. I ended up crawling on my hands and knees, all mixed up and not knowing what was happening, until some people found me and took me to the principal's office.

I was so drunk, but the only thing I could say to my worried mom was a plea, "Please don't give me to the orphans." The afterward events blurred into darkness, waking up at home, carried like a burden by my older brother. It was a fortunate twist, hidden behind the veil of a classmate's influential family and the quiet deal struck to protect their reputation. But for me, it meant a forced shift to another class, a stark reminder of the consequences that followed my association with the wrong crowd.

It was as if the more I tried to escape, the tighter the grip of despair became. The aftermath resulted in a sequence of punishments and consequences. My mom's stern disappointment and disciplinary measures—taking away my lifeline, my phone—felt like an added layer to my isolation. It seemed like everywhere I turned, trouble followed.

In middle school, things got really tough for me. I was dealing with all those teen things, you know, hormones and stuff. Then, one time, out of nowhere, I had this really dark thought about not wanting to live anymore. When I confessed about it to my older brother, thinking he could help, it just made things worse. He ended up telling my mom, and she got so upset that she ended up punishing me, or should I say she began whooping me. Can you believe it?

She didn't understand that I was just feeling really sad. Instead of helping me cope, she made me work. She said if I wanted new clothes, I had to earn them myself. So, at 15, I started working at my mom's restaurant or babysitting on the side just to buy some new clothes. It was like she was always finding ways to make things difficult. She even wouldn't let me shave my legs! Can you imagine going to gym class wearing shorts with hairy legs and everyone laughing at you? And her response was like, "Let them laugh. It's completely normal." But it wasn't normal for me. It felt like she was determined to make me go through everything she went through, whether it made sense or not and that, without any doubt, was very heart-wrenching for me.

High school wasn't a sanctuary either. My weight became a target for mockery. Being overweight in a place where intolerance was the norm meant becoming an easy target. Those jeers and mocking glances—they etched themselves deep within, becoming the harsh chorus to my already loud doubts.

Kids at school always found something to laugh about, especially when it came to my size. The fact that was hidden from them was that eating a lot kind of made me feel better because home didn't feel very good emotionally. It was like there was this big hole inside me that I tried to fill up with food. Yet, somewhere in that pain, a sense of defiance took root— I decided not to let others' opinions define me.

It wasn't easy, of course. The mockery seeped into my self-perception, painting a distorted image of who I was. Yet, somewhere in the torment, a seed of self-acceptance sprouted. It wasn't about conforming to their ideals anymore; it was about finding my own footing in a world that had seemed so determined to trip me up.

While their words stung, my acceptance of myself became the armor that I wore, a shield against people constant negativity. It didn't erase the pain, but it offered a glimmer of hope that I didn't have to conform to their standards to feel worthy.

High school marked a shift in my self-confidence and how I viewed myself. I reached a point where I thought, "Maybe I won't have a boyfriend because nobody would take me." Oddly enough, accepting this reality made me feel more at ease. I stopped caring as much about others' opinions, and that change brought me a newfound confidence.

There were two boys in our class who were considered handsome, and I had this close friend who lived next door and was pretty. I wanted them to date each other. Then, one of the boys said something unusual to me; he said that my friend was only good for having sex, but I was someone he'd want for a long-term relationship. It was a bit strange, but after a year of hanging out, we became a couple. He was my first boyfriend. It was surprising because I came from a difficult home with a lot of toxicity and negative patterns, and with no doubt at all, these patterns followed me in my love life as well.

I realized I was stuck in my mom's footsteps. As I remember, whenever there was a problem between me and my boyfriend, I'd just try to avoid it, just like my mom used to do with my dad. It also reminded me of the times when she'd drive us to a freezing lake house as punishment to my dad, thinking it would affect him. But truth be told, it didn't. All of this appeared to trap me in a toxic cycle of imitating my mom's behavior.

Continuing my relationship, I always tried to look for arguments. I had reservations about physical intimacy due to my insecurities, so I took my time in that aspect of the relationship. Nonetheless, I became the chaotic one in my relationship.

On the other hand, I wanted people to notice me, but it often ended up not working out so well. I'd make friends, but they didn't last. I was so focused on getting attention that I missed out on making real, deep friendships. It felt like a cycle: I wanted attention, but that got in the way of having strong, genuine connections. It was tough because I didn't get the emotional support I needed, and it affected how I connected with others.

I realized I was missing out on what really makes friendships special. I was so focused on getting noticed that I forgot about things like understanding, caring, and being there for each other. I learned that the emptiness I felt couldn't be fixed with just a lot of attention or surface-level friendships. Real happiness comes from having friendships that feel deep and really mean something, where you care about each other's feelings and support one another.

In one of those moments, I found myself again at that dark intersection, where hopelessness seemed to be the only way out. I remember vividly trying to escape it all with a handful of pills, wanting to numb the pain that felt unbearable. Yet, in the midst of my despair, my best friend intervened, plucking away the pills before they could overtake my state of mind. That was a turning point. It prompted a decision, a flicker of hope amidst the shadows. It was then that I applied to be a babysitter in America, a chance at something different, something distant.

But before this change came to fruition, high school felt like a constant escape, an escape from a four-walled boundary (home) where I felt stuck and like I didn't fit in there. There were times when I found myself deciding to leave home but ended up coming back as I had nowhere to stay.

Then arrived those days when I didn't have anywhere else to go except for those weekends at my cousin's place, a good distance from home. It felt different there. My cousin, her dad, and his wife made me feel safe. They were like my safe spot in the middle of all the tough stuff.

At their place, something as simple as a shared meal felt like a revelation, a source of peace. A mother offering breakfast, lunch, and dinner, a display of care I had never known. It was not normal to me, yet it appeared so profoundly comforting. I craved that sense of warmth, that feeling of being cherished. I would revel in those moments and relish in the affection that had been missing from my life. Her continuous questions like "Hey, do you want some water?" "Do you want something?"   or "Do you want to do anything?" made me realize what the true meaning of the word "home" was. So, I told my aunt she was so much more than my mother, and that unleashed a storm.

My mother, in her own psychological dilemma, couldn't comprehend my affection for someone who showed me the love and kindness she never seemed capable of. Their clash resulted in her forbidding my visits, forbidding me from relishing the only taste of motherly affection I had ever known. She barred me from a space where I felt safe, loved, and seen, all because she couldn't bear the thought of someone else stepping into the role she had failed at.

Despite her attempts to finish those ties, those weekends remained crystal clear in my memory. They were my solace, my refuge from a turbulent home. And in those stolen moments, I found a glimpse of what familial warmth felt like, something that had eluded me for so long. The love and care I received during those visits were like a balm to my bruised spirit, a reminder that amidst the chaos, pockets of tenderness do exist.

After all of these life events and the completion of my high school, I made a bold decision to pursue my lifelong dream of going to America. So, I stepped into the uncharted territory of relationships, wrestling with my insecurities and fighting the patterns of a toxic upbringing. As high school drew to a close, with all the chaos, a flicker of a dream emerged—a decision to chase a long-held desire, a journey that led me toward a new horizon: America.

Chapter Three
From Bullying To Belonging: Navigating Self-Acceptance In Adolescence

Finding self-acceptance in high school was a big deal for me. You know, high school was like a battlefield—a place where being different wasn't always cool. People there didn't always understand or accept me for who I was. Bullying? It was a pretty huge part of my life. But you know what? I found a way to deal with it. If someone tried to bully me, I didn't just take it quietly. No way. I'd roast them right back, quick and sharp. Made them feel embarrassed on the spot. That gave me a little bit of confidence, you know? They'd back off because they were scared I'd come back at them. But that wasn't exactly acceptance. It was more like defending myself.

You see, high school wasn't just about homework and classes for me. It was about figuring out where I fit in, or if I even fit in at all. Sometimes, it felt like I was different, and being different was like having a target on my back. People didn't always get me, and that made them pick on me. But I wasn't the type to just take it. Nah! If someone tried to make fun of me, I'd fire right back with something that made them stop and think twice.

For me, it was more like survival. I didn't want to be the target, so I had to defend myself. It was like putting up a shield to keep the bullies away. Sure, it gave me a bit of confidence knowing I could defend myself, but deep down, it wasn't about them accepting me—it was about me not letting their words get to me. It was about protecting myself from feeling bad about who I was.

In high school, everyone's trying to fit in, right? We all want to be part of a group, to feel like we belong somewhere. But for some of us, that's tougher than for others. I wanted that too, you know, to feel like I belonged. But it was hard when people kept making fun of me.

Back then, I didn't really understand that accepting myself was more than just firing back at bullies. It was about feeling okay with who I was without needing anyone else's approval. I wish I had known that back then. It might've made things a little easier.

You know, self-acceptance isn't just about dealing with bullies. It's about feeling good about who you are, inside and out. It's about saying, "Hey, I'm okay just the way I am, and I don't need anyone's approval for that."

I completely understand that high school is tough for a lot of people. We're all trying to figure things out at this stage. For me, it was about finding a way to cope with the teasing and the bullying. But I wish I knew then what I know now—that self-acceptance isn't about shutting people up; it's about feeling good about yourself from the inside, no matter what anyone else says.

During the disturbing years of my adolescence, there were instances where unexpected places became my source of belonging, offering solace and contributing significantly to my sense of self-worth. These were the hidden moments that quietly whispered acceptance, reshaping my understanding of confidence and belonging.

Growing up in an environment where chaos seemed routine and acceptance was a foreign concept, I yearned for spaces that would offer peace from the constant disturbance in my home. It wasn't just about seeking a temporary escape; it was about finding places where I could be myself without fear or judgment, places that would nurture my spirit and uplift my self-esteem.

One such unexpected refuge was discovered; it was an unexpected source of solace when I took the work of being a nanny. Engaging in acts of service created an unexpected sense of fulfillment. It wasn't just about lending a helping hand; it was about being part of something bigger than myself. This job instilled in me a sense of warmth and empathy, offering an environment where acceptance wasn't dependent upon societal approvals.

These moments of peace in unexpected places were transformative. They didn't just provide temporary relief; they became a source of a huge shift in how I perceived myself and the world around me. They instilled in me the realization that acceptance and confidence weren't just limited to external validations but could rise from the depths of genuine connections and shared passions.

In the calm embrace of these unexpected havens, I discovered a renewed sense of self-worth. It was here that I began to shed the layers of insecurity and self-doubt that had been weighing me down. The acceptance I found in these spaces wasn't fleeting; it was enduring, shaping my perception of self and offering a beacon of hope at the peak of adversities.

These sources of unexpected acceptance and peace served as a stark contrast to my disruptive past. They were not merely a way out from the chaos; they were integral to my journey of self-discovery and empowerment. During these unexpected sanctuaries, I found the courage to embrace my authentic self, free from the shackles of societal pressures and the weight of past experiences. They were the guiding lights that led me toward a path of self-acceptance, reminding me that amidst the noise of the world, genuine acceptance often emerges from the most unexpected corners.

In these special places, I began feeling stronger and more sure of who I was. It was like finding an anchor in the stormy sea of life. These experiences made me question a lot of things, especially the way society looks at people.

Not to mention, growing up, it felt like there was a rulebook everyone had to follow. There were all these expectations about how you should look, behave, or even feel. But being part of the drama club and volunteering at the shelter, it was like breaking free from those rules. It showed me that there's no one way to be, look, or act. We're all different, and that's what makes us cool.

I realized that society has these ideas about what's normal and what's not. It's like fitting everyone into these little boxes. If you don't fit into those boxes, people might judge you or make you feel like you're not good enough. But my experiences with people made me see that these boxes were made-up things. They weren't real.

It later got me questioning everything I'd been told about what was 'normal' or 'beautiful'. Why did we have to follow these set patterns? Who decides what's good or bad? I began challenging these thoughts and the beliefs I'd grown up with. It felt liberating, like breaking free from invisible chains.

Before, I used to feel like I had to be a certain way to fit in or to be accepted. But these experiences made me realize that fitting in shouldn't mean losing yourself. It's okay to stand out, to be different. In fact, it's pretty awesome!

Embracing my individuality didn't mean I had to rebel against everything or everyone. It was more about accepting myself fully without trying to be someone else. It was about understanding that we're all unique, and that's what makes the world interesting.

Slowly, I started to appreciate my differences. I saw that my experiences, my quirks, and even my struggles were what made me who I was. They were part of my story, and I didn't need to hide them or change them to fit in.

It wasn't an overnight transformation. It was a journey, a series of moments and realizations that changed how I saw the world and myself in it. I started to challenge those ideas of 'normal' and 'perfect'. Instead, I began to celebrate the diversity in people and in myself.

This shift in perspective wasn't just about me. It was about realizing that everyone's journey is unique. We're all on our own paths, and that's beautiful. It's about respecting and accepting each other for who we are without judging or trying to fit people into those tiny boxes.

So, these events marked a turning point – a shift from trying to fit into society's mold to embracing my uniqueness and challenging those norms that limit us. It's about standing tall and being okay with being different, knowing that individuality is a strength, not a weakness!

Chapter Four
From Poland To America: A Story Of Sacrifice And Resilience

My childhood dream was as simple as it was grand: *to set foot in America.* I can still hear the echoes of innocent conversations with friends when we were just small kids, dreaming big dreams. Back then, New York was the ultimate destination, although I imagined something warmer.

Fast forward to 2007, my fate helped me achieve and fulfill my dream. It was the result of my long planning and a leap of faith. As the final echoes of high school faded, I embarked on a journey that later reshaped my life—my travel to America.

For me, it wasn't just about going to America; it was about becoming a nanny—an au pair, as they call it—in 2007. The decision meant leaving my boyfriend behind, a sacrifice that felt necessary for the pursuit of my dreams.

That summer, right after saying my goodbyes to high school, I found myself on a plane bound for New York, more precisely, Albany. It was the start of a whole new adventure. Two kids and a decent family—this was the deal that would provide me with both a visa and an immersive experience of American life.

Arriving in America, the land of my childhood dreams, was an exhilarating experience. The energy of New York filled me with a sense of accomplishment. Becoming a nanny in 2007, I felt like I was living the dream my friend and I had cherished as small kids. I spent three months there, and during my time there, I decided to visit Massachusetts with the host family.

With its charming scenery, Massachusetts became more than just a pretty view. It turned into a stage where relationships and self-discovery played out, setting the scene for the experiences that awaited me, like an opening act to the larger story of my life.

As the crisp Massachusetts air kissed my face, I found myself in the company of newfound friends and familiar faces. Among them was a guy, a connection I hadn't fully grasped the significance of at the time. Innocent exchanges and occasional calls set the stage for a connection that later became something more important.

In the midst of my time there, I came across a trio of Polish friends—two guys and a girl. The dynamics, however, took an unexpected turn. The girl, though adorned with beauty and in great shape, harbored a tinge of jealousy toward me. It wasn't about appearances but rather the conversations that took place. The guys, drawn to my communication style, unwittingly fueled her envy.

Growing up with two brothers in the same room had grown a natural ease in communicating with guys inside me. It wasn't about superiority; it was the comfort of familiarity. Little did I realize that this simple dynamic would set the stage for subtle tensions among our newfound friendships. The following weeks in New York turned out to be a set of different emotions and connections.

However, the initial excitement waned as I found myself in upstate New York, a place not quite aligned with my dreams of warmth. The reality of the job as a live-in nanny brought a unique set of challenges. While the family and the two kids were manageable, the monotony of everyday life set in. Boredom crept in, fueled by a restlessness that had been a constant companion throughout my life.

The impact of my past toxic relationship and the toxic environment of my upbringing lingered, leaving an indelible mark on my ability to form healthy connections. As I settled into my new life in New York, the weight of the past bore down on me. The scars of emotional turmoil had not faded; they merely found a new place in my foreign surroundings.

It wasn't just about adapting to a new culture; it was about confronting the ghosts of unresolved issues that haunted my past. The patterns of running away, ingrained during harsh times at home, manifested in my interpersonal relationships. The fear of facing conflicts directly, the instinct to flee when confronted with challenges—these are fragments of a coping mechanism forged in the intense heat of past traumas.

In the pursuit of stability and self-discovery, I grappled with the repercussions of my toxic relationship. The echoes of arguments, the emotional instability, and the constant need to escape situations at the first sign of conflict persisted. It was as if the past had strained my entire being, affecting my present and dictating my responses.

Forming genuine connections became a delicate dance, a tightrope walk between the yearning for connection and the fear of vulnerability. Trust, the cornerstone of healthy relationships, became elusive. The wounds of past betrayals and the constant upheaval of my upbringing created an invisible barrier, making it challenging to let others in.

The newfound stability in America brought with it the opportunity for introspection. As I reflected on my journey, I realized that the same patterns that played out in my family, the same inclination to run from problems, had seeped into my own life. The lake house escapades mirrored my tendency to escape emotional turmoil, even if it meant leaving others behind.

The impact of past trauma wasn't confined to my romantic relationships alone. It reverberated in every aspect of my life, influencing my decisions and interactions. The fear of being tied down and the restlessness that fueled impulsive decisions, all stemmed from the unresolved issues that I carried with me across borders.

My decision to return to Poland wasn't a sudden one but a gradual realization born out of a sense of stagnation. The twelve-month contract seemed like an eternity, and after just three months, I succumbed to the restlessness.

When I mentioned the idea of returning to Poland to my friend, who was already jealous of me, she kept pushing me, insinuating that if I could afford college in Poland or had a boyfriend, I would undoubtedly go back. Despite college in Poland often being free or reasonably priced, it seemed like she was trying to play mind games with me. Eventually, I made the decision to return, holding onto the false hope that my family would welcome me back with open arms.

After three months, I found myself back home. Boredom and a longing for the chaotic life I was used to, in contrast to the calm with the host family, led me back. My boyfriend also urged me to return. However, my family's response was far from supportive. They laughed at me, labeled me a loser, and claimed they knew I would come back because I was weak. The regret of returning to Poland weighed heavily on me.

I remember the internal struggle torn between the lure of America and the familiarity of home. The impulsive decision to cut short the contract was met with mixed reactions.

Returning home, I was met with zero support. The old car my mother had given me was gone, sold off while I was away. The lack of familial backing and the absence of personal transportation left me relying on my own legs to navigate life once again. Yet, during these challenges, a resilient determination began to take root within me.

Realizing the gravity of my decision, I regretted the premature termination of the opportunity that represented my childhood dream. My family's judgment lingered, echoing in my ears. The laughter and the name-calling branded me as a failure, a nobody.

However, adversity has a peculiar way of strengthening the spirit. I knew I had to do whatever it took to return to the land of dreams. It was a turning point, a moment of self-reflection that set me on a path to redeem the missed opportunity.

Back in Poland, the disapproving laughter of family members followed me. They questioned my choices, labeled me a failure, and even sold the car my mom gave me—a symbolic act signaling that I wouldn't be coming back.

Undeterred, I was determined to correct my course. College became a temporary distraction while I bided my time, waiting for the moment to embark on the journey back to America. But academia couldn't compete with the magnetic pull of the land of dreams.

Yet, the allure of America remained strong within me. Determined to rewrite my narrative, I found another opportunity, another chance to pursue my American dream. However, this pursuit came with its own set of challenges. Waiting for the visa, I worked tirelessly as a nanny and house cleaner, determined to save every penny. The financial struggles were compounded by strained familial relationships, with my mother withholding support due to her perception of a previously wasted opportunity.

My journey toward America was not a linear path. It was marked by the resilience forged through years of labor starting at the age of 15.

Working as a weekend nanny during my teenage years, I earned money to escape the judgment associated with my clothing choices. This early initiation into the workforce laid the groundwork for the relentless pursuit of my dreams.

Working as a nanny, engaging in various odd jobs, and saving every penny became my daily routine. The strained relationship with my boyfriend and the absence of financial support from my mother were additional hurdles. The echoes of past patterns—of running away from problems—remained, but a newfound determination pushed me forward.

The echoes of my mother's expectations reflected through the relationship and reinforced a sense of inadequacy.

As I continued to work and save, I confronted the shadows of my past, including an initial moment with my first boyfriend. I recall a moment from my time with my first boyfriend. After a while, we found ourselves facing the unsettling situation of a condom breakdown, and I was around 18 at that time. In my unease, I confided in him, and he, in turn, involved his mother, who happened to work at a pharmacy. The immediate response was a swift acquisition of a Plan B pill.

Without much regard for my own feelings on the matter, they insisted I take it. The message was clear: if I wanted to continue the relationship, I had to take this step immediately. I complied, but the aftermath left me grappling with a wave of guilt. The weight of being young and navigating such complex situations added an extra layer to the discomfort, leaving me with a lingering sense of unease.

These challenges, mixed with familial patterns, toxic relationships, and a relentless pursuit of dreams, set the stage for the next chapter—an exploration of strength, self-discovery, and the pursuit of fulfillment on American soil.

As the year and a half waiting period loomed, I persevered. The sacrifices, the odd jobs, and the emotional upheavals were all stepping stones on the path back to America. It was during this time that the complexity of relationships unfolded, adding layers to my journey—a journey marked by strength, determination, and a relentless pursuit of dreams on foreign soil.

During the hustle of my daily routine, I noticed recurring patterns from my past—tendencies to avoid problems rather than confront them. These echoes were fragments of a familial legacy, a script passed down through generations.

Yet, during these struggles, there was a glimmer of hope. The awareness of these patterns, and the acknowledgment of the scars, was the first step towards healing. In the foreign land where dreams were meant to come true, I found myself on a parallel journey—one of unraveling the layers of past trauma, understanding their impact, and gradually rewriting the narrative of my life.

The journey was far from over, but with each step, I moved toward a version of myself free from the shackles of the past. The echoes of trauma may have shaped my journey, but they wouldn't define its destination.

The longing for America persisted, and as the waiting game for the visa played out, I toiled relentlessly. The hurdles were more than financial; they were emotional, figuring out strained relationships and overcoming judgments. My journey to America in 2009 marked not just a physical relocation but a profound transformation, a narrative poised for the next captivating chapters of my life.

As I reflect on the disruptive journey from my childhood dream to the realities of adulthood, it's like unraveling a story filled with sacrifice and self-discovery. Deciding to face my toxic relationship and explore a foreign land became a crucible for personal growth. The challenges weren't solely financial or emotional; they were the crucibles where strength was forged and determination solidified.

As I embarked on this journey, the pursuit of the American dream became more than just moving across geographies. It became a pilgrimage into the depths of my own mind, confronting demons and embracing vulnerability. The terrain of my experiences, marked by highs and lows, resembled the uneven landscapes of life itself.

Returning to America in 2009 wasn't just about changing my physical location; it marked a profound transformation within me.

Now, standing at the doorway of introspection and personal growth, I realize that the journey isn't a straightforward progression. It's a blend of disappointments and victories, heartbreaks, and moments of pure joy. The recognition of past patterns and their influence acts as a guiding compass, directing me toward a future free from the constraints of family history.

Chapter Five
Finding Strength In Vulnerability: Navigating Toxic Relationships

When I pursued my dream of going to America, I decided to leave my boyfriend. Passing through the complexities of leaving behind a toxic relationship to embark on a new journey in a foreign land was a challenging part. The toxicity in my relationships mirrored patterns deeply ingrained in my family dynamics. Like my mother, we were conditioned to run away from problems rather than confront them.

This pattern became glaringly evident during our family's retreats to a lake house. The retreats weren't about cozy family bonding; they were desperate attempts to escape conflicts. The rustic lake house lacked basic amenities like heating, plumbing, or insulation. Winter nights were endured in jackets and blankets as we sought refuge from unresolved issues between my mom with my dad.

And guess what happened to all of us? We all were running away from the problems. We developed the same pattern: whenever we had problems in our relationship, instead of just sitting down and talking about it, we chose to run away. And that's what I was doing in my relationship.

In moments of strife, I found solace in running away, using it as a coping mechanism. My response to arguments was to immerse myself in self-destructive behavior, often seeking refuge in my car. It became a symbol of instability, a vessel for transporting my unresolved issues.

This cycle of escape and confrontation continued in my toxic relationship. Arguments with my boyfriend triggered an instinct to flee, seeking refuge in the familiar confines of my car. It was a tumultuous cycle of conflict and escape, mirroring the patterns of my family history.

The relationship itself became a source of distress. My boyfriend's criticisms about my weight triggered a profound emotional impact, crushing my self-esteem.

During his criticism, I reached a crucial realization. I understood that my self-worth shouldn't be determined by someone else's opinions or judgments. It dawned on me that true happiness and confidence come from within, not from seeking validation in the eyes of others.

I embarked on a journey of self-discovery, learning to appreciate and love myself for who I am, irrespective of external perceptions. Embracing my uniqueness and quirks became my strength. I discovered that the key to genuine happiness lies in self-acceptance and understanding that I am more than enough just as I am.

Motivated by this newfound perspective, I started prioritizing my mental and emotional well-being. I let go of the toxic notion that my value hinged on conforming to someone else's expectations. Instead, I focused on nurturing a positive self-image, recognizing the beauty in my imperfections, and celebrating my individuality.

Over time, I developed a strong sense of self-worth. The criticisms that once crushed my self-esteem became mere echoes, overshadowed by the empowering belief that I am in control of my happiness. This shift in mindset marked a turning point, allowing me to break free from the shackles of external judgments and embrace the liberating journey of self-love.

Other than that, as I stand here and reflect on my past, coming back to Poland was a turning point in my journey. It meant facing the echoes of my past and understanding how my time in America had shaped me. This return wasn't just about a shift of the place; rather, it was about digging into the deep-seated issues that had defined my life.

My hometown, with its familiar streets, brought a rush of emotions—both good and bad. The judgments and laughter of family members still lingered, refusing to fade away. But during all these criticisms, a strong determination began to take hold. The decision to cut short my American dream had been met with skepticism, yet I refused to let it define me. Adversity, I discovered, had a way of making me stronger.

Back in Poland, I found myself caught between the allure of America and the comfort of home. The impulsive decision to return left me questioning if I had made the right choice. College became a way to pass the time while waiting for the right moment to go back to America. Yet, the pull of the land of dreams was hard to resist, and relationships added complexity to my journey, marked by strength and a relentless pursuit of dreams.

As I faced the challenges of daily life, I saw recurring patterns from my past—avoiding problems rather than confronting them. These echoes were fragments of a family legacy. Yet, within these struggles, there was hope. Recognizing these patterns and acknowledging the scars became the first step toward healing.

Returning to Poland wasn't a step backward; it was a pause for introspection and self-discovery. The disapproval of others labeled me a failure, but I refused to accept that perception. It became a moment of self-reflection, pushing me to redeem the missed opportunity.

Reflecting on my journey, I unraveled a story filled with sacrifice and self-discovery. The challenges were more than just financial or emotional; they were crucibles where strength was forged. The recognition of past patterns guided me toward a future free from family constraints.

The beginning of this journey toward self-discovery and healing is a universal tale, inviting those facing similar challenges to find solace in the shared human experience of overcoming adversity and believing in the possibility of a better life.

My experiences, though personal, mirror the struggles many face in life. It's a shared journey of confronting demons, embracing vulnerability, and finding the strength to rewrite my narrative. As I grappled with my roots and the haunting trauma, a newfound determination emerged—not just for personal redemption but to inspire others to believe in a brighter tomorrow.

Chapter Six
Against All Odds: Rebuilding Life's Foundations In Pursuit Of Dreams

Back in Poland, as I returned to the familiar yet unknown landscape of my home country, a message from an older guy in the USA brought an unexpected interruption to my daily routine. In a life where attention from others was a rare occurrence, his message brought a small but significant ray of joy into my wort was an unexpected spark, a momentary brightness in a life that often felt dimly lit.

During those moments, I didn't really get what his message meant. I wasn't thinking much about the complicated stuff in human relationships, especially emotions and desires. It didn't matter to me if he wanted sex as I was far in Poland. What really mattered was that someone noticed me, gave me attention, and made me feel seen—even if it was just for a short while.

My self-esteem, already fragile from past relationship struggles, felt comfort in the attention he gave me. Just the feeling of being wanted, even if I didn't fully understand his motives, offered a brief escape from the self-doubt that haunted me. Without a strong sense of self-worth, any form of acknowledgment became valuable, no matter the real intentions behind it.

Thinking back on those moments, I can clearly see how much my self-esteem was broken. It's almost hard to believe how far I had fallen, being ready to be with anyone just to have someone around, to feel noticed and recognized, even if it was only on a surface level.

In the midst of my ongoing struggle with inner challenges, the guy from the USA kept in touch, overcoming the distance with occasional calls and messages. By this point, my relationship with my boyfriend had changed, and he knew about this new connection. Open communication was essential; I made it clear that our interactions were focused on practicing English and having a friendly chat.

Engaging in meaningful conversations in English, a language I hadn't completely mastered, felt like a bit of a challenge. Still, our talks were uncomplicated—we'd inquire about each other's lives, share experiences in Poland, and contemplate the prospect of returning to the USA. It served as a vital connection, surpassing the limitations of distance that kept us apart.

In the bigger picture, our conversations were quite normal, lacking any evident romantic undertones. While my English skills weren't extraordinary, the authenticity of our talks went beyond language barriers. These conversations acted as a lifeline, keeping me connected to a world beyond the immediate struggles in my surroundings.

My current boyfriend, at that time, knew I was trying to learn English for a friend back in the USA, but it didn't bother me.

The time I spent in Poland after coming back from the USA gave me some time to reflect on how much I didn't want to stay back home. The echoes of my mother's laughter, the jeers, and the demeaning labels thrown my way by my own family etched wounds deeper than I could have ever imagined. According to them, my return was not just a physical homecoming but proof of all my character's weaknesses.

My mother, in her moments of mockery, declared that I couldn't even accomplish the simple act of staying in the USA. The weight of her words, laden with ridicule, was unbearable. I felt like I was being punished for seeking peace of mind back in my roots. The relentless name-calling and the laughter that seemed to reverberate through the walls pushed me to the edge.

Unable to cope with the emotional disturbance, I sought refuge in food—a silent companion that never judged. As my emotions spiraled, so did the numbers on the weight machine. The once-kind and nice person I knew myself to be became the target of unwarranted comments and insensitive remarks. It was during a harsh moment, cooking with my boyfriend at his house, that the weight of judgment bore down on me.

His mother's scrutinizing gaze, paired with a cutting remark—"How much do you have to eat?"—pierced through my fragile defenses. In that kitchen, I crumbled, retreating upstairs to let tears escape my eyes. The cruelty of those words, delivered without empathy, intensified the internal struggle. I grappled with the question of why people could be so harsh, especially when my coping mechanism, my source of peace, was not harming anyone else.

Those interactions served as a powerful reminder that my struggles weren't just with external challenges but also with my internalized sense of self-worth. In those vulnerable moments, haunted by hurtful words, I held onto the belief that one day, I'd liberate myself from the chains of judgment, emerging stronger and embracing the person I was meant to be.

Opening up to my mom about my struggles, her response was harsh: "You're fat, eating too much. Work and buy your own food. I won't spend my money on you, especially now that you're 18." It triggered memories of when, at 15, I worked not to support the family but because my mom wouldn't buy me clothes. Instead of getting me new clothes, I was left with my sister's hand-me-downs—clothes from a bygone era, a throwback to '80s fashion. Those words, instead of offering understanding or support, felt like a harsh judgment.

During this absurdity, one simple desire remained unchanged—to be loved. No matter how challenging my mom made things, the yearning for unconditional love persisted. Even amid the chaos, I clung to the hope that, someday, I'd find the love I'd been searching for all my life.

My unquenchable thirst for my mother's validation persisted, a longing that seemed insatiable no matter how hard I tried. Months of relentless work and saving finally paid off when a company agreed to sponsor my return to the USA. Boarding the flight with only $20 in my pocket, having spent $10,000 on the program, I faced the challenge of rebuilding my life from scratch.

When I sought help from my mother, desperate for support, I was met with a resounding refusal. "I'm not making this mistake again. You'll be back anyway," she declared callously. It echoed the past, a pattern of abandonment. In 2007, she sold my car during my first trip to the USA. Now, in 2009, she gave away half of the house to my brother, which included my room and bathroom. I found myself without a place to call home.

With determination burning in my heart, I made a solemn vow to myself: no matter how challenging, I was staying. There was nothing left for me back in Poland. The ties that once bound me were severed, and I faced the daunting task of starting anew in a land that held both dreams and challenges. The journey back to America became more than just a physical relocation; it was a strong tale of strength and the pursuit of one's dreams against all odds.

And so, I embarked on the journey once again, securing a visa as an au pair and landing in New Jersey. The host family, a blend of a Polish mother and a Dutch father, seemed like an opportunity to continue pursuing my dreams. Little did I know the seemingly simple job would turn into a challenging ordeal.

The Polish mother, with an overwhelming case of OCD, had additional tasks for me – cleaning and cooking for extra money. Given the meager weekly income of $180, an extra $50 was a welcome relief. However, I soon realized that the extra cash came at the cost of becoming her Cinderella.

My responsibilities extended beyond childcare; I found myself cleaning floors on my knees, changing bed sheets daily, and preparing elaborate Polish dinners that consumed a significant amount of time. Balancing these chores while keeping an eye on her 2-year-old daughter proved to be a Herculean task.

Despite my efforts, a month into my stay, I faced an unexpected dismissal. The reason? Talking on Skype during my working hours. It happened during the little one's naptime, which I believed to be my moment to catch up on cleaning. The abrupt termination left me shattered. The fear of returning to Poland, a place void of support and understanding, loomed over me like a haunting specter.

Caught in between the uncertainty, my family at home and the company that brought me to the U.S. were placing bets on how long I'd stay this time. Returning to Poland wasn't an option I was willing to entertain. As the company scrambled to find me a new host family, they granted me a mere two weeks to secure a solution.

Despite these challenges, my determination to thrive in America stood tall. This was the proof that I was growing to be strong in the face of adversity. The skepticism and bets cast by my family, questioning my ability to succeed, only fueled the fire within me. I refused to be confined by the limitations others impose, driven by a profound belief in my capacity to shape my destiny.

As I went through the complexities of adulthood, it became evident how profoundly my childhood experiences shaped my present. The echoes of my parents' behavior resonate in the emotional struggles I face today. The scars of their judgments and abandonment are engraved deep within, influencing the way I perceive myself and others. Yet, with introspection and self-awareness, I strive to break free from the chains of the past, forging a path toward emotional healing and personal growth.

In my life, every thread, no matter how tangled or frayed, told a story of strong character and self-discovery. I stand at the intersection of past and present, acknowledging the impact of my journey on the person I've become. My resolve to create a life filled with purpose and authenticity remains unshaken, a beacon guiding me through the shadows of doubt toward a brighter, self-defined future.

Chapter Seven
From Betrayal To Breakthrough: Overcoming Obstacles In A Foreign Land

In the face of adversity, even when things got tough, I stayed strong and didn't let life's challenges bring me down. The echoes of family troubles and harsh judgments from people I cared about stayed with me, but instead of giving up, they pushed me to keep going and build a better life in the USA.

Returning to Poland after my initial American adventure had been met with ridicule and skepticism. Family members, placing bets on my perceived failure, laughed at my dreams. The fear of surrendering to their judgment and the haunting memories of past family trauma urged me to keep going in the USA.

During all this chaos, I shared my feelings with the guy I met in 2007. He proved to be a supportive presence, flying down to New Jersey to spend a weekend with me. Naively, I believed our connection was blossoming into a romantic relationship, as I envisioned him becoming my future boyfriend.

During his visit, I overheard him having a conversation on the phone, casually saying to someone, "I love you too." Puzzled, I questioned the unusual exchange, only to be told it was his sister on the other end. In my youthful innocence, I accepted the explanation with a simple, "Oh, okay, that's cool." Little did I know, this was just a glimpse into the complexities of relationships and the unexpected turns they could take.

The two weeks of uncertainty wore on, and with no new host family in sight, the guy from Massachusetts, who had now become my confidant, took matters into his own hands. He drove down to New Jersey, determined to rescue me from the looming uncertainty. Together, we made our way to Cape Cod, where he arranged a place for me to rent with a Russian girl.

In my hopeful innocence, I believed that the guy would be more than just a supportive friend. I envisioned a romantic connection, longing for someone to love me the way I yearned to be loved. However, reality struck hard when I discovered that he had a girlfriend, someone he lived with, and I was merely a side attraction.

A few days before starting a job at the gas station, the company called and inquired if I was still in the USA. I affirmed, and to my delight, they informed me that I had been matched with a family in Orlando, Florida. Tears of happiness streamed down my face as I realized I wouldn't have to stay in Cape Cod, especially after learning about the guy's secret relationship. My discovery of his girlfriend, uncovered through the social media platform "MySpace," painted a picture of a life he had hidden from me, leaving me both disappointed and relieved.

In Orlando, a fresh start awaited me, and I embraced the opportunity with newfound determination. My host family provided a welcoming atmosphere, and despite the recent turbulence in my personal life, I was ready to focus on my responsibilities as an au pair.

Meanwhile, the guy's web of deception became more apparent. He had concealed a significant detail from me: a considerable age gap between him and his girlfriend, a revelation that blindsided me. Despite the shock, I felt compelled to reveal the truth to her, sensing the dishonesty that lingered in the air.

Meeting his younger girlfriend, I shared the unfiltered reality, hoping that honesty would set her free. Grateful for the transparency, she initially distanced herself from him. However, the complexities of relationships often defy simple solutions, and over time, she chose to return to him.

Embarking on my dream in Orlando meant relinquishing the pursuit of a warmer climate. I decided not to let my age define me—no longer sticking to the notion that being 20 meant I didn't know what to do with my life. Despite the whispers of a troubled home and the fear of returning and facing judgment, I pressed on, supported by the knowledge that many shared my struggle.

Rather than allowing the past to dictate my path, I embraced the uncertainty. The choice wasn't between having sex with a stranger to merely stay desired or returning home to scornful laughter and judgment. It was about recognizing that my journey was not a solitary one; countless others faced similar challenges in their pursuit of something more. The decision to push forward, to reach for a dream in Orlando, became a witness to my strength and the shared struggles of those seeking a better life.

During my travel journey to Orlando, I made a stop with a guy I knew. Surprisingly, I encountered a kind Jamaican family, friends of his, who extended their help. They turned out to be incredibly nice people. The mother, in an unexpected act of generosity, hosted me for a few days before my flight from Boston to Orlando. She even drove me to Boston. This unexpected support came at a crucial moment, providing me with the encouragement and assistance I needed during a challenging time.

Their assistance was a gesture of compassion, born out of sympathy for my situation. However, I always held the belief that I am the captain of my own ship, steering my life in the direction I choose. I've never been one to embrace victimhood or complain about the challenges life throws my way. Every time I faced adversity, I allowed myself a day to shed tears, and the very next day, I emerged stronger.

I've never allowed myself to dwell in self-pity or let others feel sorry for me. The kindness they showed in helping me move to Orlando through the company was appreciated, but I carried with me the motivation and determination to face whatever lay ahead. My approach to life has always been to confront challenges head-on, turning tears into strength and emerging ready for the next chapter. That was my mantra!

Our life often mirrors our inner state, and when you're filled with mental and emotional trauma, you tend to attract similar energies. This was evident in the family I worked for – a household where the mother seemed to carry unhealed wounds. The stresses of managing kids, household chores, and occasional outbursts mirrored the environment I grew up in. However, it wasn't as severe, and there was at least an act of discipline, something lacking in my own home.

I committed to the entire contract period with this family, unsure of what awaited me afterward. During this phase, a silver lining appeared in the form of a fellow Polish friend, also a nanny. Born in the same year, we quickly became inseparable and remain best friends to this day. Together, we went through the challenges of our respective roles, finding peace in each other's company.

Despite the difficulties with the family I worked for, the companionship of my newfound friend brought joy and a sense of belonging. We shared not only the responsibilities of our jobs but also moments of celebration and amusement. This period of my life was marked by forging lasting connections and finding strength in the company of someone who understood the unique challenges we were facing as nannies far from home.

There is no doubt that in this country, that was far lost from my life – confidence. Even in situations where a guy's intentions were merely physical, the acknowledgment that someone desired you, especially when you battle insecurities, provides a boost in confidence. Whether or not one chooses to engage, the simple fact that someone finds you desirable contributes to a sense of self-assurance. This starkly contrasts with my image back in Poland, where the cruel society often seems to dictate that overweight women are not viewed as desirable partners.

Here, the experience, even if limited to the physical, played a significant role in building my overall confidence. Stepping out into the world, I carried a newfound assurance in myself. It wasn't about conforming to certain standards; it was about embracing the validation, no matter its form, and allowing it to shape a positive perception of self. This shift marked a turning point in my journey, where external experiences began molding a stronger and more confident version of myself.

Rejecting advances from guys, even though my confidence was growing, couldn't shield me from the looming concern of an expiring visa. As the deadline approached, worry crept in, making me question what my next steps would be and how I could extend my stay.

Just when I thought things were taking a positive turn, my friend, who had become like family, got married and joined the military. Once again, I found myself all alone. This feeling of being lonely was attacking my senses just when I thought I had found a true friend; her life changed and she had to move out!

In the midst of this loneliness, I encountered a guy who seemed promising. He gave me a hope of a quick marriage. To me, this seemed a chance to be together, which indirectly uplifted my spirits. However, reality struck hard when he not only stole money from my account but also vanished without a trace. The betrayal left me fighting with both emotional and financial wounds, a harsh reminder that even in the pursuit of love, one could come across unexpected heartbreaks.

Locating him for a divorce became an unrestful quest, leaving me entangled in the marriage for three agonizing years. The hurdle lay in securing a foreign lawyer, a financial burden that disturbed my path to legal freedom.

In the initial weeks of our marriage, he was working in a car wash place, and I was hunting for a nanny job. However, financial struggles haunted our household, aggravated by his spending on marijuana. The dire situation forced me to take extreme measures, limiting my meals to once a day to stretch the available resources.

A turning point emerged when my ex-boss, concerned about my visibly degrading health, intervened. Recognizing the unhealthy environment I was trapped in, she took matters into her own hands. Against my initial resistance, she insisted I move in with her, a decision that ultimately saved my life for good.

It was during this transition that I discovered a significant blow—my ex-husband had withdrawn $1500 from my account. While the amount might seem modest to some, in my vulnerable financial state, it left me virtually penniless. The revelation served as a stark wake-up call, prompting me to confront the harsh realities of my past choices and their impact on my present circumstances.

The money he took was saved for crucial immigration papers, an investment in my pursuit of legal employment and stability. Despite the setback, my ex-boss, recognizing the urgency of my situation, graciously opened her home to me. Her offer was simple—assist with household chores and childcare in exchange for a place to stay. It felt like a lifeline during all those chunks of chaos.

During my two-month stay, I gathered the courage to apply for jobs, eventually landing a position with a single dad. His disruptive past included a divorced wife, now imprisoned and bereft of custody. He rented a room in someone else's house, claiming to be a pilot mechanic with frequent work-related travels. Yet, his financial struggles were evident; he took various loans, which left him with nothing but a 'no-cash' state.

Desperation led me to tolerate unfavorable work conditions. Despite the ongoing situation, I was determined to establish my independence. The job, however, turned out to be a disappointment. The supposed pilot mechanic failed to pay me for six weeks of labor, leaving me in quite a vulnerable position. This experience underscored the harsh realities of my journey—a struggle for financial stability in an unfamiliar land fraught with disappointments and challenges.

We relocated to a house in Satellite Beach, adjacent to Cocoa Beach. However, the move was far from glamorous—we entered an empty house devoid of furniture, resorting to sleeping on air mattresses. Despite the less-than-ideal living conditions, I found peace in the fact that I was far away from the toxic environment of my past.

The struggles persisted, but the thought of returning home was never an option I entertained. I kept my challenges hidden, a choice reinforced by a past incident when I sought financial help from my family. The response was dismissive, a reminder that my decision to come to America was my own and that I should face its challenges independently. The acknowledgment of my strength, albeit from an unexpected source, fueled my determination to persevere, even in the face of adversity.

The challenges continued, and my family's response to my struggles only intensified my resolve to prove them wrong. Determined to overcome the hurdles, I decided to change jobs and secured a position in West Palm Beach. This time, I worked for a stay-at-home mom who was expecting twins. However, our differences in religious beliefs became apparent when she expected me to work on Christmas, a holiday I held dear as a Catholic.

Despite the clash of traditions, I persevered, determined to create a stable life for myself in the USA. The job change allowed me to continue forging my path in a foreign land, overcoming challenges one step at a time.

The clash of traditions became apparent when my new employer, a stay-at-home mom expecting twins, expected me to work on Christmas. As a Catholic, this holiday held special significance for me. When I questioned her decision, she explained that it was for her neighbors, who were Catholic, and she wanted to host a Christmas party.

This situation reminded me of my mom, who was always concerned about what others would think. It struck me how she, like my employer, overlooked the importance of family and the value of personal connections. Despite the differences, Christmas remained a cherished holiday for me—a time to feel needed and find comfort in the company of family and friends.

As I think back on the Christmas episode with my employer and the clash of traditions, I'm starting to wonder if my mom's extravagant displays of affection on that day were just an act. It occurred to me that she might be really good at pretending to be loving, especially during holidays, making it seem like she genuinely cares when it could all be just a show.

Despite the job change, my interest in partying remained alive. Weekends were a blur of blind dates and social gatherings driven by a deep-seated desire for attention. Throughout my life, I had always been the one loving others, but the concept of being genuinely loved by the other person remained elusive. Like my mom, I sought attention, yearning to understand the true essence of love.

I kept looking for attention, and I found myself going on blind dates and hanging out with friends. Simple things like having dinner or watching a movie became ways for me to get the attention I didn't get at home. Since I didn't get much recognition while growing up, I always felt like I needed to keep searching for it.

After my stint in West Palm Beach, I found employment in Hollywood, Florida. The lady I worked for mirrored my mother in emotional volatility. Despite the challenges, my attachment to her children kept me with the family for several years—three or four, to be precise. The workload was substantial, but the love I felt for the kids compelled me to endure.

I kept up with my job, working six days and nights a week. I only had one day off, from Saturday noon to Sunday 6:00 p.m. It was a short break in the never-ending routine. I felt a strong connection to the kids I worked with because I understood the emptiness they felt at home, having gone through something similar myself.

Staying with them for an extended period, perhaps, was my way of bridging the gap. The act of their emotions mirrored what I had witnessed in my own home. My mother, much like my employer, was always out partying, leaving the children yearning for her presence. My boss was often absent, similar to my mother, but it didn't affect the kids as much. Unlike other bosses, she rarely let her moods affect me—maybe occasionally, but never to the point where it was unbearable.

In this new environment, I found the freedom to be myself. Dating, partying – my boss never passed judgment. Perhaps, being divorced herself, she understood the need for personal space and exploration.

However, as time passed, I realized that one night off and half a day wasn't sufficient, especially in my twenties. So, I made a move to another family's home. Though the setting was somewhat dull, they had a guest house. The prospect of having my own space was enticing.

Yet, the family's expectations were different. The mother, a stay-at-home mom with four children, had a specific vision in mind for the person she wanted around. The journey continued each phase, revealing new challenges and opportunities for me.

Her focus was more on maintaining the cleanliness of the house than on spending time with her own kids. Daily tasks included cleaning the bathrooms and floors. Although I was capable of cleaning, my strength lay in connecting with the kids. Over time, the boredom set in as I found myself alone without a car in a dull city.

Feeling the need for a change, I reached out to a friend I had met during my nanny program classes in New York. To my interest, she offered me a job in New York. The desire for a more happening and lively environment, with opportunities to socialize and enjoy life, fueled my decision to explore new possibilities.

When I first flew in, I stayed with her for a few days as we figured out the ins and outs of the nanny program. We decided to be roommates. She lived in the city of New York, and the idea of living there seemed like a thrilling adventure. So, without hesitation, I left the warmth of my beautiful state for the hustle and bustle of New York City.

Excited about moving to New York with my friend, I had no idea it would bring more challenging times. Despite the city's energy and chances, challenges were waiting for me. Little did I know, my new room would turn out to be no bigger than a closet, with a window facing the next building. The warmth of my old state felt far away, and now, in the city that never sleeps, I was about to face unexpected difficulties.

Chapter Eight
Unforeseen Challenges: A Rollercoaster Ride Of New Beginnings

Life sometimes presents us with opportunities for a fresh start, and it's human nature to be drawn to the idea of every new beginning. Every human tends to jump on it without thinking of any consequences. All that life has to do is give us a chance to change things up, experience something different, and explore unknown territories, and we get convinced. I found myself doing just a similar thing when I decided to switch cities for a job.

The promise of a different life was too tempting to resist, and little did I know that this seemingly spontaneous choice brought thousands of unexpected turns and twists into my life. I knew that life's invitations for a fresh beginning could be both exciting and unpredictable; what I didn't know was that my experience would become a reminder of the unexpected adventure that would open many uncharted chapters in my life.

I still remember November when I made the move to NYC. My body, used to the warmth of Florida, hated the cold even more. The living situation was also not much better. My roommate and I shared a small apartment with another friend of hers. My room was nothing but a short closet with no space to fit in.

My room was so small that the moment I opened my door, it collided with my full twin-size bed. I hated this feeling! To make some room for storage, I had to buy bookshelves so that a makeshift place could be made for my clothes. Why did I do it, you ask? The answer is quite simple: it was all that I could afford at $750 a month. Life was as sad as baring the unwanted cold weather in New York City.

Enduring the harsh reality of New York, I secured a job as a live-out nanny. At that time, I didn't know that this position would uncover a series of abuse in my life. Despite my inherent kindness and lack of boundaries, I found myself working 12-hour days for a meager $650 weekly wage. Life was indeed getting harder and harder! In those days, anyone with a sense of justice would argue or fight for themselves that such demanding hours should result in at least a grand. However, the reality differed, and my monthly paychecks became the harsh reality of the hindered economic agendas.

To add a layer of complexity, I took on an extra gig to assist a friend of my roommate. Watching a 13-year-old boy for an additional two hours after my primary job became a routine. But I didn't know that doing this would turn these two days a week into an extremely demanding 14-hour workday. The schedule was tiring – from 6 am to 11 pm, my life was turning into a never-ending loop of work and commute. I was becoming sleep-deprived!

The strain on both my physical and mental well-being was becoming unbearable. During all this chaos, exhaustion became my constant companion, making me irritated and frustrated. The sheer monotony of my days began to wear on my senses. Each step felt heavier, each hour longer, and the weight of my responsibilities seemed unfulfilled. In a few days, I turned into a living puppet of the New York hustle, pushing my limits just to make ends meet.

In a city that never sleeps, my own rest became a rare entity. As my body yearned for peace, my mind demanded an escape from the relentless mode of my life. One day, frustrated by the fatigue and boredom of my life, I turned to online dating. I did it so that a ray of excitement could be introduced to my otherwise dull and boring life. The glow of the screen offered a brief escape from the harsh realities of my life. It gave me a fleeting moment of connection in a world that seemed indifferent to my struggles.

The dates, however, were far from fairy tales. They became fragments of time when I tried to regain my sense of belonging. I did it to find happiness between the busy hours of work and sleep. The attractions of the city, once enticing, now became a harsh reality. My efforts to figure out the maze between the subway stations and bustling streets in search of calm and peace turned me really exhausted.

The beauties of the city lights, which were once really attractive to me, were now turning dull. They all were worn out! The closeness of a demanding job and the need for personal happiness created a very disturbing environment for me. I wasn't able to figure out what was right and what was not. Yet, in the chaos of it all, I clung to the hope that each day brought me closer to a reality where my efforts would indeed be rewarded. I also hope that the city will soon begin to compensate for all the wounds that it was giving me!

Between the frustration of exhaustion and monotony, the desire for change burned bright within me. The city that had initially seemed like an unforgiving force now became the place where I started developing a sense of strength within me. I continued to face the challenges of my daily life with a glimmer of determination and dedication. I made a silent promise to myself that the struggles endured would not go in vain.

In the hustle and bustle of New York City, where the tired working hours and constant struggles can easily wear down the beats of one's heart, I found pace in unforeseen places. It was across the river in New Jersey. As someone who had embraced the unpredictable nature of blind dates back in Florida, the notion of meeting new people wasn't new to me. However, I didn't know that this encounter would later become the core reason for so many unexpected events in my life.

With time, I was thinking that my quest for more and something new was increasing with each passing day. I was expecting something new from my life. It was in those moments that I began yearning for meaningful connections, conversations that exceeded the superficial, and perhaps, a companion who would share the enthusiasm of life with the same energy as mine. Money had never been the main attraction for me; rather, it was the prospect of engaging in smart, stimulating conversations that captured my attention.

As the city lights gleamed and the days turned into long weeks of work and duties, I found a rare connection with someone at a long distance from me. It was a guy living in New Jersey. My initial intention was casual. All I wanted was a friend with benefits, a fleeting escape from the routines that had become the major chunk of my days. Little did I know that this encounter would turn into an unexpected chain of events.

My conversations with this guy quickly turned into a delightful exchange of gestures. It was something very different than usual for me. My idea of a friend with benefits quickly evolved into something more. We decided to meet, and as our eyes met for the first time, there was an undeniable attraction that set the tone for what was to come. Something more than just friendship!

The chemistry between us was irresistible. Even I was a bit shocked that what began as a casual fling took an unforeseen turn after our first intimate meeting. Unexpectedly, he expressed a desire for more, dismissing our initial idea of being 'friends with benefits.' In that moment, as the city lights twinkled in the distance, I felt a shift. This shift was felt in the trajectory of my life as if the universe had finally decided to align the stars in my favor and I was really happy.

Despite the long distance between us, we managed to stay in touch and give our relationship a chance of turning into something big. With each passing day, all my weekends became symbols of love, with either him crossing the river to my small apartment in the heart of NYC or me going to the suburbs of New Jersey. The routine of our weekends became a source of joy. It was as if we were escaping from the monotony of our lives together. The thing which was in my favor: *we both wanted the same things!*

There was a contagious excitement that began reflecting in my being. It was a feeling of contentment, a sense that perhaps I was about to get free from my long-lived, torturous life. My life was finally turning in the right direction where I might finally find happiness. The relationship brought a sense of fulfillment, a phase of my life that contrasted starkly with the struggles and uncertainties that had defined my recent past.

For the first time in a long while, the shadows of my previous life problems seemed to disappear into the background. The city that had witnessed my relentless pursuit of stability and happiness now bore witness to a new chapter – a chapter marked by love, companionship, and the promise of a future that sparkled with hope.

As we went through the complexities of a long-distance relationship, the enthusiasm that covered us became our guiding light. Our weekend meetings became more than just dates. They became the celebration of our happily forged connections and proof that love can find its way even when two destined people live way across from each other.

In those moments, as we carved out our own haven between all of life's chaos, I couldn't help but feel a profound gratitude for the unexpected twist that life had thrown my way. I was very happy that with each passing day, the city that once made me agonizing was now offering from both hands. And it wasn't just anything; it was joy, complete joy! I started cherishing moments of laughter and began sharing the secrets of a couple living in the simple joys of companionship. Little did I know that the bridges connecting New York and New Jersey would become the symbols of something much bigger than the mere concept of true love!

My love life was turning into something more than perfect, but my work life was witnessing huge struggles. After six months of tirelessly working, I reached a breaking point and decided to quit my job. It seemed like I could never find the right fit for my heart, always giving so much and receiving too little in return. A woman in Long Island, who happened to be a friend of my ex-boss in Florida, offered me a position as a live-in nanny. What I didn't know back then was that this new job would bring about another set of challenges, as my kindness seemed to be a trait others took advantage of.

This woman knew me through my ex-boss, her best friend. Knowing my naïve nature, she figured out that I was an easy target to manipulate. They were in the process of building a house, so they temporarily stayed with her parents-in-law. To my surprise, I found myself sharing a room with a 7-year-old girl. The arrangement was never mentioned beforehand, leaving me a bit uncomfortable with this unexpected turn of events.

My decision to seek employment in Long Island was driven by a desire for a quieter environment than the bustling chaos of NYC. Because, let's be honest, my nature never quite aligned with my lifestyle. However, the new job brought its own challenges. Every weekend, I went on a two-hour train journey to visit my boyfriend, as having him over was not feasible due to his living arrangements. And let me tell you, the understanding of this situation didn't make the separation any easier.

Reflecting on my experiences as a nanny, I couldn't shake the feeling that something might be wrong with me or that landing a stable and fulfilling job was an unattainable feat. The pattern of unfavorable working conditions began to take a toll on my confidence, leaving me questioning my worth and capabilities. Yes, it was true! I started questioning myself.

Juggling between these demanding jobs not only affected my professional life but also hindered my ability to dedicate time to my long-distance relationship. The strain of commuting and long working hours left little room for nurturing the connection with my boyfriend. And our weekends together became the only source of peace from the challenges that overshadowed my workweek.

During all these struggles, I only relied on my boyfriend, who remained a pillar of understanding and encouragement to me. Despite the hurdles, our relationship blossomed, proving to be a source of strength in the face of professional uncertainties. Little did I know that these challenges were preparing me for something greater, teaching me the power of strength and the importance of holding onto relationships that truly matter.

It was after 10 months into our relationship that an unexpected twist occurred—I found out I was pregnant. The news wasn't at all planned, and fear gripped me at the thought of sharing it with my boyfriend. To my surprise, when I finally gathered the courage to tell him, he reacted with overwhelming joy and excitement about becoming a father. That gave me a huge relief! Too eager to share the news, he promptly informed his family during one of our weekend visits, and their collective enthusiasm added to our joyous moment. It was indeed the best day of my life!

Empowered by this support, I made the decision to quit my existing job and move in with my boyfriend and his family. This was the only way to remain cautious at that time! Transitioning to a new phase of my life, I secured a job in New Jersey with a welcoming Turkish family.

All the living arrangements in my child's to-be Dad mirrored the warmth I had always envisioned. It was a small apartment with three bedrooms and one bathroom, accommodating his parents, his older brother on the couch downstairs, another brother with his wife and child, and, of course, my boyfriend and me. Despite the close quarters, the prospect of having a supportive and caring family around me filled me with happiness.

As time swiftly passed, I found myself two months into the pregnancy. Life was finally turning good! However, an unexpected challenge emerged out of nowhere as I began experiencing excruciatingly painful cramps. Oh my God! The pain!!! Concerned, my boyfriend's older brother expressed that such pain during pregnancy didn't seem normal. Despite the discomfort, I decided to wait and observe.

Three days later, unable to endure the persistent cramps any longer, I decided to seek medical attention. The visit to the hospital uncovered a harsh reality that later tormented the blissful world I had been building. The joy of nurturing parenthood was suddenly overshadowed by the discovery of a distressing and unimagined complication.

For me, in those initial moments of realization, the support of my boyfriend and his family became more crucial than ever. What had initially been a period of excitement and relief—quitting my job to embrace impending parenthood—now transformed into a time of difficulty and concern. I knew that the path ahead was uncertain, but the unmatched support from my loved ones became my source of strength in the storm. Little did I know that this event was about to turn my newly happy life into something unbearable!

Chapter Nine
Shattered Dreams: Navigating Loss And Loneliness

Life has this way of throwing curveballs just when you think everything is falling into place.

You could be on the verge of what you believe are the best times of your life, and suddenly, things take a harsh turn, flipping your world upside down. It's like standing on the edge of a cliff, ready to embrace the view, and then the ground beneath you suddenly shifts away. The journey can be unexpectedly tough, leaving you fighting with challenges you never saw coming. It's a reminder that life is unpredictable, and the highs and lows can hit you when you least expect it.

During the midst of what seemed like the best times of my life, life decided to throw me a curveball that left me in a situation where I thought everything was about to end. Just when I believed I was on the brink of happiness, unexpected challenges hit me, and I found myself dealing with a reality I never imagined to pass through. It felt like standing on that cliff again, only this time, the fall was even more daunting.

In those moments, it's easy to feel like life won't offer any hope for a happy future. The challenges can be so overwhelming that you question if you'll ever see the light at the end of the tunnel. It's like going through a storm, unsure if there's a calm harbor waiting on the other side. Yet, in the face of these hardships, it becomes crucial to remember that life's journey is filled with twists and turns and that time never remains the same!

Just as I once thought my life was about to crumble, I later discovered that there were unexpected opportunities and new beginnings waiting for me. Even when it seems like the darkest hour, there's a chance for a sunrise. It's a reminder that strength and hope can emerge from the most challenging situations, offering a path forward even when it feels like all hope is lost. Always remember that life's journey is unpredictable, and sometimes, unexpected hardships pave the way for surprising moments of strength and growth.

Okay, going back to the day when I finally arrived for my first doctor's appointment. Accompanied by my boyfriend and his mom, I entered the doctor's office with a lot of questions in my mind. The process had been delayed as I was facing the complexities of no insurance. As I lay on the examination table, thousands of sorts of thoughts filled my mind. All that I could think of was the joy I felt when I first heard about my unborn child.

However, within the span of a 10-minute ultrasound and the insights of two doctors, my hopeful expectations were shattered. Shattered completely! I still remember their words hung in the air: ***"There is no baby inside."*** It was the day when I got to know that instead what should have been a developing fetus was an empty embryo. The news hit me like a tidal wave, and I struggled to understand the cruel reality unfolding before my eyes. The excruciating cramps that had plagued me were not signs of a healthy pregnancy but rather my body's attempt to tell me that all my dreams were close to breaking.

It was the day when I wasn't able to control my overwhelming emotions. I still remember that I wept uncontrollably that day. Inside, I was trying to fight with the unfairness of it all. I began questioning myself: *Why did this have to happen?* The positive thoughts I had tried to foster now seemed distant, replaced by the harsh truth that this pregnancy was not meant to be. As I exited the doctor's office, tears streamed down my face. It was a visible manifestation of the emotional dilemma that my soul was trying to distinguish.

Walking away from that experience, I carried not only the weight of the immediate loss but also the resurgence of past traumas. The news triggered memories of a life marked by adversity, a history of challenges that had shaped the person I had become. The pain was not only physical but echoed the deep emotional scars that had defined my journey.

On the other hand, my boyfriend was dealing with his shock as well. Silence was the element he was sticking to. But his presence there gave me a sense of peace. The unspoken understanding between us acknowledged our shared grief, and together, we were about to face the aftermath of our torn hopes.

With time, my physical pain intensified. It was a sheer reminder of the body's natural response to an unviable pregnancy. Each cramp yelled the emotional disruption and multiplied the constant distress. I was torn inside! The journey that had begun with hope and excitement now turned into a painful chapter of loss and sadness.

In the aftermath of this heart-wrenching revelation, I clung to the belief that, somehow, this painful experience was part of a larger, yet unknown, plan. As I confronted the depth of sorrow, I also found strength within, drawing from the sweet support of my loved ones. Together, we faced the harsh reality of a dream deferred, clinging to the hope that, with time, healing would prevail.

As the date for my surgery approached, I found myself dipped in a mixture of anxiety and frustration. The surgery was scheduled two weeks after the devastating news of my empty embryo. It aimed to remove the unviable remains of my baby, as my body hadn't miscarried naturally.

On the day of the surgery, my boyfriend's mom accompanied me to the hospital, providing me with a reassuring presence and support. I thought that everything would eventually be okay after the surgery. Doctors told me that they would discharge me on the same day but just after a few days of my surgery. This way, I will have a brief recovery period before I can return home. However, at that moment, I wasn't familiar with the fact that this medical intervention would make me see many real faces.

As I lay on the hospital bed, the preoperative preparations began happening around me. A nurse delivered a reassuring message, *"You won't remember me, but I'll be with you during the surgery."* Despite the attempt to instill calm, there was an undercurrent of fear that gripped me. The prospect of undergoing surgery was terrifying, but I clung to the hope that it would bring closure to this painful chain of events.

For me, the transition to the operating room was a surreal experience. The clinical sterility of the environment heightened my vulnerability, and anxiety coursed through my veins. With my boyfriend at work, his mom stood as my pillar of support, accompanying me into the unknown.

The moment arrived when they gave me anesthesia, promising that everything would be fine once I got up. As the drug took effect, the boundaries of wakefulness blurred, and I slipped into a deep sleep. However, this unconsciousness was short-lived, and I soon woke up to a reality that shook me to my very core.

The post-surgery awakening was far from the expected reality. I found myself screaming in pain, a stark contrast to what the nurse told me. Blood stained my legs, a disturbing sight that blurred the image between expectation and reality. It was nothing but devastating!!

In my distress, I communicated the intensity of the pain to the medical staff, expecting they would assist me. However, their response was disconcertingly indifferent as if they were attempting to normalize an abnormal situation. The expressions on their faces betrayed a different truth – this was not the typical aftermath of such a procedure.

Despite the pain and the unsettling circumstances, I tried to gather all the courage in my stamina to face the turn of events. To me, each moment was a test of strength, an unanticipated challenge that demanded both physical and emotional fortitude. In facing the unexpected aftermath of the surgery, I displayed a trait of a strong character that was born out of necessity but for my own betterment.

As the extent of my internal screams calmed down and was replaced by a profound sense of discomfort, I began collecting myself.

There was no doubt that the aftermath of the surgery left me in a state of vulnerability, both physically and emotionally. After enduring the painful procedure, all I wanted was the comfort of home. But I was unaware of the fact that this wish would leave me frightened and empty-handed.

As I gradually regained consciousness in the recovery room, I was deeply saddened by the absence of familiar faces. The medical staff assured me that my boyfriend's mother had been contacted to take me home. But it was a reassurance that quickly turned into disappointment when she failed to answer their calls. Abandoned in the painful environment of the hospital, I felt a profound sense of abandonment.

Unable to rely on the pre-surgery support, I reached for my phone. I was desperate for a connection that could fulfill my growing sense of isolation. Dialing my boyfriend's number, I poured out my distress, questioning why nobody seemed to care for me in this moment of need. His response, however, added another layer to the heartache. It was so distressing.

He calmly informed me that he would be able to come after finishing work in approximately 30 minutes. The idea of enduring this post-surgery loneliness for another half-hour felt like an eternity. Overwhelmed with emotion, I implored him to come sooner, emphasizing the urgency of my need for companionship. Yet, his response lacked the empathy I sought.

"I will come after work. Talk to you later," he declared before abruptly ending the call. The abruptness of his voice left me shattered, feeling abandoned not only by his mother but now by him as well. The vulnerability I felt after the surgery was now compounded by a profound sense of loneliness, a stark contrast to the support I had yearned for.

The passing minutes seemed eternity as I waited for his arrival. Unable to contain my growing distress, I reached out to him once again, inquiring about the delay. His response, seemingly trivial, further fueled my despair. He explained that he needed to change out of his work clothes before heading to the hospital. This was an explanation that felt inadequate to me, given the circumstances.

I felt that his choice of attire was unwanted compared to the emotional turbulence I was going through. A simple pair of sweatpants from work should not have been a barrier to his immediate presence, especially when my plea for companionship echoed with urgency. As the minutes ticked away, my surroundings became a disheartening reminder of the emotional vacuum that surrounded me.

When he finally arrived, the relief was overshadowed by the anguish that had accumulated during his absence. The physical pain from the surgery seemed dwarfed by the emotional toll of feeling abandoned at a time when I needed reassurance the most. The scars left by that solitary experience lingered long after the physical wounds had healed. They engraved a painful memory of vulnerability and longing on my soul.

Returning home after the events at the hospital, I looked for a ray of hope and a sense of peace in the company of my boyfriend. However, he rejected my request to lay together with an unexpected response. To my dismay, he retreated downstairs to engage himself in video games, leaving me alone in my emotional turmoil.

The weight of the situation bore down on me, and I couldn't contain the flood of tears that covered me. The one person I sought comfort from had become emotionally distant. The contrast between my vulnerability and his choice to escape into virtual realms intensified the sense of isolation.

Seeking distraction, I returned to work the following day. Surprisingly, my boss, sensing my distress, offered words of solace. In a calm and reassuring manner, she reminded me of my youth and assured me that everything in life transpires for a reason. Her kindness and supportive words provided a glimmer of hope amid the emotional turbulence, encouraging me to believe in the inherent purpose of life's twists and turns.

After going through the tough time of losing the pregnancy and feeling disconnected from my boyfriend, I decided to take control of my life. A few months later, I went to visit friends in Florida and realized that there was nothing for me in New Jersey. The relationship had lost its meaning, and the state felt unwelcoming. Gathering all my courage, I made the tough choice to break free from the unfulfilling relationship and the suffocating atmosphere of New Jersey.

I returned to Florida, seeking comfort in a familiar place. I found a job caring for the children of a lawyer's parents in a really spacious house. This job not only brought stability but also provided a peaceful environment. It gave me hope and the belief that I could rebuild my life in a place that felt like home.

Choosing to go back to Florida was a turning point for me. I knew it was the place where I could regain my sense of self and find peace in a supportive setting

Chapter Ten
Pedaling Through Heartbreak: Finding Strength In Solitude

Discovering a job that offered self-sufficiency, I felt something that was long gone from my life – *hope*. At that time, I was craving for a turning point in my life. It was to bring a sense of independence that I desperately needed at that time.

With this sense of satisfaction, I started my nanny job with great determination. After several months of being employed for the children of the lawyer's parents, it dawned on me that they were just the wealthier versions of my own parents, minus the alcohol consumption. The family was completely tormented. The mother appeared to show a typical discontent nature, with nothing ever satisfying her. Meanwhile, the father portrayed a stereotypical image of a snob, incessantly discussing wealth and blabbering about his rich father, who had previously married a stripper.

In the ordinary setting of the kitchen, a moment of utter terror happened that left me shaken to my very core. The kid's dad's gaze disgusted me as I innocently sipped juice through a straw. To his guts, the man, without warning, uttered words that turned the air sour. "I can tell you like to suck," he said, a crude remark that struck me with shock and nothing but anger.

Despite the unsettling feeling, I tried to gather the strength to respond firmly. I warned him that if he repeated this disgusting behavior at any time sooner, I would run to his wife and explain all his inappropriate comments to her. In those moments, fear of his unsavory intentions clashed with my determination to stand my ground. The silence that followed marked a small victory for me as it ensured me that he would never dare to make such remarks again!

During all the hustle of my daily routine, my ex-boyfriend continuously reached out to me, pleading for a second chance. Eventually, I surrendered to his pleas and granted him an opportunity for a long-distance relationship, with no intention of returning to New Jersey.

Our relationship settled into a monthly weekend visit, alternating between him coming to me and me flying out. August brought a unique circumstance; my understanding bosses, aware of the challenges of a long-distance relationship, generously allowed him to stay with me in their house during their vacation to look after their dog.

The decision to reconnect outbreak a bunch of emotions and contemplations. Uncertainty and hope persisted as I moved forward with the complexities of reviving a relationship. It was way more difficult than I thought, given the challenges posed by geographical distances. The idea of periodic reunions brought both peace and longing, a balanced interchange between the joy of togetherness and the agony of separation.

The decision to connect our lives again was not taken lightly, as it involved leaving the pain of the past against the potential of a new beginning. I still remember that these moments were filled with self-doubt as I went through the storm of emotions. I began questioning myself whether the heart could find its way back to trust and love once more. The challenge of maintaining a connection across miles became a prominent thought, emphasizing the importance of communication and understanding. And I was all up for it!

Each visit, both fleeting and precious, held the promise of rekindling the flame and bridging the gaps created by distance. In the silent moments, I became used to gathering all the resilience required for a long-distance relationship. Recognizing that it demanded more than just affection, we both tried to start a shared commitment to overcome the hurdles that geographical separation presented before us. This phase of reconnection burned like a flame due to a hopeful heart, ever cautious yet willing to explore the potential of love beating the odds of distance.

When my boyfriend came to visit me in Florida, I felt happy. Introducing him to Florida quite excited me, but I sensed his reluctance. There was an instance when I felt he was kind of hiding the fact that he was dating me again from his family and friends. This event occurred while cooking dinner. His phone rang, and he hurriedly answered in a foreign language, running toward a distant corner. Although many questions arose in my mind, I tried to dismiss them. Ignoring things was my familiar pattern from past toxic relationships.

This stirred up feelings of insignificance inside me, and I began reflecting on past experiences. Instances like these started hinting at deeper issues, whether embarrassment or a communication barrier, leaving me questioning my own worth. I began doubting myself. It made me wonder if my appearance played a role—did my boyfriend avoid acknowledging our relationship because he thought others wouldn't find me attractive? This question fueled the emotional turmoil, intensifying my struggle for acceptance and understanding in relationships.

Embarking on a vacation with high hopes, I found myself shouldering the financial burden with an empty wallet while my boyfriend visited. To my surprise, upon his departure, the bitter truth surfaced—he had been unfaithful to me. This betrayal marked the end of our relationship. Determined to heal, I turned to a simple yet therapeutic outlet: *biking*. The music and melodies in my ears became a source of peace for me, helping me in my recovery process.

Ending the relationship demanded strength—breaking free from toxic cycles and prioritizing personal well-being. It was a journey fraught with challenges, yet each pedal stroke became a source of reclaiming control over my life. Reflecting on this period of self-discovery, the lessons learned loomed large. Putting an end to a relationship stained by dishonesty and betrayal was an important step toward renewing my identity and fostering a healthier mindset.

Figuring out the complexities of heartbreak, the bike rides became a source of amusement to me. The wind against my face mirrored the disturbance within, but with every passing mile, I distanced myself from the pain. The importance of setting boundaries and recognizing red flags took center stage in my newfound journey toward strength. Riding through the emotional landscape, I embraced the reality that self-worth should never be compromised for the sake of a relationship. ANY RELATIONSHIP!!!

During the ocean of disappointment, the solitude on those bike rides nurtured self-sufficiency. Each turn of the wheels was a symbolic act of moving forward, leaving behind the emotional baggage. The playlist reflected the evolving emotions within me—songs of heartbreak gradually transforming into anthems of empowerment.

The strength to end the relationship came not from vengeance but from a commitment to my own well-being. It signified breaking free from the shackles of a toxic past and embracing the offerings of a brighter, self-defined future. With each tear leaving the eye, the emotions became the guideposts for future relationships, emphasizing the importance of mutual respect, honesty, and emotional well-being.

In the aftermath of heartbreak, the bike rides continued, not just as a means of escape but as a declaration of strong determination and self-love. The journey toward healing was a testament to the enduring spirit within. It was a spirit capable of overcoming betrayals, learning from the past, and ultimately, emerging stronger.

However, my reliance on others persisted, and the void in my life led me to explore online dating. The intention wasn't to find a soulmate but rather to distract me with conversations and attention. It was a temporary remedy for my wounded heart. In this pursuit, I encountered another guy.

As I tried to put my interest into this new connection, the process of rebuilding life after the second breakup began. The initial interactions were a blend of uncertainty and hope, each message carrying the weight of past experiences. Yet, in the quest for healing, these conversations played a role in redirecting my focus, if only temporarily.

The importance of embracing independence and self-love gradually became evident. The online meet-ups served as a mirror reflecting the need to nurture one's individuality. It wasn't about finding inner peace in the company of others but, instead, seeking solace within oneself. Yeah, that's deep! This realization marked an important moment in my journey toward self-discovery.

Going through the landscape of post-breakup healing, I discovered the importance of self-love. The online dating escapade, initially driven by a desire for distraction, transformed into a platform for self-discovery. Interactions with new people fostered a sense of independence within me. The independence that had long been overshadowed.

As I engaged with these new connections, the need to rely on external affirmations came to the forefront. The process of rebuilding my love life wasn't merely about finding a new companion; it was an internal reconstruction. The newfound understanding of self-worth became the cornerstone of forging healthier connections in the future.

My life after the second breakup was uncovered in the space of digital conversations. The online dating venture, initially a distraction, evolved into a catalyst for self-reliance. It was becoming a platform where I could write my story from scratch and to my own satisfaction!

Self-love is important, and it should be taken care of by every individual. The temporary happiness derived from online connections served as a stepping stone toward a more profound understanding of self. It wasn't about seeking validation externally but, rather, recognizing the strength that comes from within.

After another terrible heartbreak, the journey toward healing became quite difficult for me. The second chance at connection became a first step toward rediscovering the uncharted territories of self-love, independence, and the profound ability to stand strong on one's own. I took it as a challenge, ready to discover my instincts!

Chapter Eleven
Transforming Pain Into Power: A Journey Towards Self-Discovery And Empowerment

I want to take some time out and reflect on my past relationships and how they shaped my personal growth before going to the other chapter of my life. I still remember that life threw challenges my way, but through them, I discovered a new me. More profound and even stronger!

In the mess of toxic relationships, I found strength, pure strength! The toxic patterns stuck around, but I became tougher. There's a saying that *we often attract what we think we deserve,* and looking back, I think my *"settle for the bare minimum"* mindset pushed me to accept all the lows of a relationship.

My journey toward healing started by acknowledging the wounds. The wounds that were so deep that they scratched my very soul! It took courage to face the shadows of the past, break free from co-dependency, and rediscover my true self.

Each heartbreak taught me some valuable lessons. As I learned that broken trust needs time to heal, I built healthier boundaries and learned to respect myself. Recognizing that I deserved love and respect reshaped my sense of self. It brought to my mind a sense of self-assurance.

Breaking free from toxic cycles demanded courage, and in doing so, I found the necessity of self-love. Ending relationships became a matter of reclaiming my identity and embarking on a journey of self-discovery.

Let me assure you that it wasn't a solo journey. A series of supportive voices lightened my path. Friends, mentors, and genuine care became my pillars. Despite some really messed up relationships around me, I worked hard to set things straight.

The journey to self-discovery came with several challenges. Confronting fears, shedding limiting beliefs, and enjoying my own company became essential for me. In between all of this chaos, solitude became a necessary element, reconnecting me with my authentic self.

Going through post-breakup life, I discovered the beauty of independence. It wasn't about being alone but being complete within myself. And to me, it came as a beautiful life lesson. Hobbies like biking weren't just distractions; they became forms of self-care and moments of enjoying the present.

Through these life experiences, I realized that relationships reflect the connection with ourselves. Everyone must remember that to attract love, self-love must come first. My breakups display my journey from toxic entanglements to self-discovery. To me, this is a story of vulnerability, compassion, and the commitment to cultivate love from within. The journey continues, and with each step, self-growth blossoms.

Going forward with life, empowerment became the guiding force for attracting a positive future. Throughout my life hurdles, I learned it's not just about moving on, but it's about moving forward with purpose and intention. Yes! This motto can give you a clear perception.

Aspirations and goals took center stage, not just in personal but also in professional development. The lessons from my past relationships translated into a determination to create a life filled with purpose and fulfillment.

All you have to do is make sure that your journey to empowerment starts with choices. Choosing growth over stagnation, self-love over self-doubt, and strength over surrender. It's about recognizing that the power to shape my future lies within me.

For personal development, setting boundaries is a powerful tool. Learning to say no without guilt, protecting my energy, and surrounding myself with positivity was pivotal. The realization dawned that personal growth requires a deliberate commitment to oneself.

In between balancing my energy and juggling my nanny jobs, my professional development paralleled my personal growth. For me, channeling energy into meaningful work became a priority. The sense of discovering my insights meant taking risks, seeking opportunities for learning, and embracing challenges.

Throughout my life's hardships, I knew that mindset played a crucial role. Shifting from a victim mentality to one of empowerment changed the game. Instead of dwelling on past mistakes, they became stepping stones for future successes. The narrative transformed from *"Why me?"* to *"What can I learn?"*

By now, you know that my journey wasn't without hurdles, but they became stepping stones. Rejections, failures, or setbacks weren't endpoints but opportunities to pivot and grow. Every hurdle became a chance to prove myself. And I took my chances.

To me, building a life filled with purpose meant identifying passions and aligning actions with values. It meant asking profound questions: *What brings joy? What feels meaningful?* Answers to these questions became the blueprint for a fulfilling life.

My mother's neglect and my imitation of her toxic behavior in my relationship became a life-long challenge for me. But soon, I decided to see these challenges as opportunities. I began finding moments to celebrate. And by celebration, I meant celebrating successes, big or small. Each accomplishment, whether personal or professional, fueled the belief in capabilities.

Life became a canvas, and empowerment the brush. The power to shape a positive future was more than just about personal and professional goals. It was about creating a life reflective of newfound strength and wisdom.

In essence, all these complexities enabled me to witness my evolution from being the victim to victor, from being passive to empowered. It displays the journey of translating hard-earned lessons into intentional choices, aspirations, and a mindset geared toward a future filled with purpose and fulfillment. I am still in my development phase, assuring that I just learned good things from my journey.

During my breakups, building a support system became essential in figuring out life's challenges. Friends who doubled as confidants, mentors who provided guidance, and the warmth of self-sufficiency became pillars of my strength. These connections were not a sign of weakness but a celebration of shared human experiences.

The journey taught me the significance of healthy relationships. Toxic patterns were replaced with connections that nurtured growth. It was about choosing relationships that added value rather than detracting from them. The shift was from dependency to interdependency – a mutual exchange of support and understanding.

Independence wasn't about standing alone; it became more about standing strong on one's own terms. It was about recognizing that personal strength, coupled with a robust support system, was a formidable combination.

For me, the pursuit of happiness became a deliberate choice. It wasn't about waiting for circumstances to align but about finding joy in the present moment. It meant letting go of what couldn't be controlled and focusing on what could – personal growth, relationships, and self-love.

Healthy connections became the bedrock of a fulfilling life. It was not about the number of relationships but the quality. I learned that nurturing connections that align with values and contribute positively to life must become the new norm.

My lifelong journey underscored that independence doesn't mean detachment. It's the freedom to be authentic, to make choices aligned with personal values, and to go through life's challenges with hope. For me, the embrace of independence was more than just a solo act. It was a collaborative mix of personal strengths and a support system.

In essence, my life's difficulties taught me the transformative power of embracing independence. It narrates the shift from dependence to interdependence, emphasizing the value of personal strength and the role of a robust support system in the pursuit of happiness. My journey continues as a testament to the evolving understanding that true independence is not a solitary journey but a collective embrace of strength, connections, and the pursuit of joy.

Reflecting on the significance of this journey, it becomes apparent that self-discovery is more than a destination; it is an ongoing process. As my life continued revealing layers of difficulties, I began sticking by the sense of strength, growth, and the relentless pursuit of a fulfilling existence.

For me, optimism became the driving force, a companion in facing all life's uncertainties. The ability to find hope amid challenges emerged as a skill cultivated through the highs and lows. The anticipation for the future wasn't clouded by fear but fueled by the understanding that every twist and turn was an opportunity for growth. This mindset helped me see myself grow.

Remember, growth is not confined to a particular phase but a continuous evolution. It is quite evident in the subtle shifts in perspective, the newfound strength in vulnerability, and the ability to embrace change. Growth is synonymous with adaptability, a key component in the journey toward a fulfilling life.

The continuous journey toward fulfillment is not a linear path. It involved detours, pauses, and moments of reflection. It is about savoring the present while holding aspirations for the future. Moreover, fulfillment is not a distant goal but an intrinsic part of the everyday choices made on this journey.

In conclusion, the reflection on this transformative journey offers me the essence of optimism, anticipation for the future, and final thoughts on the importance of growth. My ongoing process of self-discovery reveals that fulfillment is not a destination but an ever-present companion. My lifelong story is an example of 'strength' and 'hope' embedded in the human spirit and the continuous pursuit of a life rich in meaning and satisfaction.

All of these traits enabled me to continue my life and put myself ahead on a dating platform. For me, it meant that I was ready to take on new challenges and that I wasn't afraid of any unplanned difficulty that life planned to throw my way forward.

Chapter Twelve
Unexpected Connections: A Journey Of Curiosity And Compromise

When faced with the aftermath of a difficult breakup, the decision to re-enter the dating zone was both daunting and liberating for me. It's important that one must figure out his own challenges before seeking solace in someone else's arms.

As my heart continued to heal, I found myself considering dating as a way to move forward and find hope. Initially, I viewed it as a means of distraction, a temporary escape from the pain of the past. However, as time went on, I began to see it as something more. It became an opportunity to bridge the gap between my past and the future, a chance to rediscover who I truly was in the midst of all the emotional chaos.

Dating became a way for me to explore new connections, learn more about myself, and open my heart to the possibility of love once again. It became a beacon of hope, guiding me toward a brighter and happier future.

With each new encounter, I gained valuable insights and learned important lessons about myself. It became a process of peeling back the layers of vulnerability, allowing me to be open to new experiences and connections. Building trust again was a gradual process, taking one step at a time. Each interaction taught me something new about my desires, boundaries, and the qualities I sought in a partner. It became a transformative journey, shaping me into a stronger and more self-aware individual.

The path to healing is far from a straight line; it's filled with moments of doubt and hesitation. Yet, with every date, I could feel my heart growing stronger and the wounds of the past slowly fading away. It served as a powerful reminder that resilience is born from vulnerability.

Despite the pain I had endured, love had the ability to flourish once more. Each date showed me that there were still kind and genuine individuals out there, willing to explore a connection with me. It taught me to be brave, to open myself up again, and to trust in the possibility of love. Through these experiences, I realized that healing was not about erasing the past but about embracing the lessons it had taught me.

In my online dating experience, I expected not to find anyone serious. I just hoped the attention from guys would distract me and help me heal. That's when I came across someone unexpected – an Asian guy!

He wasn't my usual type, and I never thought I'd be his, either. Being a curvy girl, I couldn't believe it when I sent him a message saying, "Did you get lost? Is this a mistake?" The idea of an Asian guy being interested in me seemed far-fetched. But my curiosity got the best of me, and we started texting.

Even though I wasn't initially attracted to him, we kept talking for three months before I agreed to meet him in person. Those months of texting created a connection I hadn't ever hoped for. We shared our hopes, dreams, and fears in the hope of providing a sense of peace to each other.

Our first meeting happened by accident. I was out with my friends, enjoying a long night, when he messaged me, asking what I was up to. In a spontaneous move, I invited him to join us at the bar. I asked him to pretend like he knew me, just so I wouldn't feel foolish in front of my friends.

But clearly, he wasn't very good at covering it up. He asked me questions that a guy would typically ask on a first date. Despite my lack of interest, we continued the evening. As we left the bar, my friend waited in the car to drive me home. That's when the unexpected happened.

He tried to kiss me. Out of nowhere, he just pulled himself on me and tried to kiss me. I immediately refused, shaking my head in disbelief. I wasn't attracted to him, neither inside nor out. There was nothing between us besides my curiosity about why he wanted me.

As I got into the car, my mind raced with questions. How did I end up in this situation? Was it my desperate attempt to heal that led me here? Little did I know this encounter would be the catalyst for a series of events that would change the course of my life.

It took another month before I gathered the courage to see him again. The attention he gave me drew me in, making me crave more. Our dates became frequent, and I found myself enjoying his sarcastic remarks. It reminded me of my upbringing, where sarcasm was a common language shared with my brothers. Perhaps it resembled the toxic environment I grew up in.

But as we grew closer, I couldn't ignore the red flags. They were waving right in front of me, signaling potential issues. However, like a well-practiced routine, I chose to ignore them, just like I did at home. In our households, emotions were suppressed, and problems were brushed aside, leaving us ill-equipped to handle them.

In hindsight, I realized that nobody had taught us how to face the complexities of emotions. I was left to take care of myself on my own, clinging to a fragile connection that seemed to offer solace from the chaos around us.

He was a college student in his late twenties, juggling his studies while chasing a scholarship. Despite his commitments, we spent every weekend together. But it was during these moments that his true colors emerged. Alcohol transformed him into a different person - careless, seeking the attention of other women, and showing no regard for my feelings.

His drunken episodes were never-ending. One night, as we drove home from the bars, I remained sober due to stomach issues. He, on the other hand, was heavily intoxicated. It was on that dark highway that everything went out of control. Suddenly, tears streamed down his face, and he yelled out that nobody liked him. In a shocking and dangerous move, he opened the car door while I was driving. I acted swiftly, grabbing hold of him and pulling him back inside. I had to keep a tight grip on his head until we reached home. This whole event left me so confused!

The next day, he calmly claimed to have no recollection of his actions, brushing it off as if last night never happened. But deep down, I knew that this incident was a manifestation of the underlying trauma he carried. It became evident that both he and I had endured challenging childhoods, and in our naivety, we believed that our shared pain would somehow translate into an extraordinary love.

Little did I know that my life would take a sudden turn. After just three months of being together, he asked me to move in with him. Desperate to escape the clutches of my bosses, I agreed without hesitation. But as soon as I settled into our new home, I received a devastating blow - I was fired from my job without any warning or explanation. I wasn't even given the chance to bid farewell to the children I had grown to love and care for over the course of a year.

The news hit me like a ton of bricks. I felt a wave of shock and disbelief wash over me, followed by a deep sense of betrayal. It was as if the ground had been ripped from beneath my feet, leaving me in a state of uncertainty and vulnerability. The sudden loss of my job left me feeling stripped of my identity and purpose. I had invested so much of myself into that position, and to have it taken away without any warning or explanation was a painful blow to my self-esteem.

As the days turned into weeks, the reality of my situation began to sink in. The financial strain started to weigh heavily on my shoulders. The fear of the unknown and the uncertainty of what the future held for me gnawed at my every thought. I felt a deep sense of shame and embarrassment, as if my worth was tied solely to my employment status.

The days stretched on, and the absence of structure and routine left me feeling adrift. I struggled with feelings of inadequacy and self-doubt. The constant questioning of my abilities and worthiness for future employment consumed my mind. I couldn't help but question whether I had made a mistake in agreeing to move in with him so quickly without securing a stable job beforehand.

The combination of losing my job and the weight of financial instability took a toll on my emotional well-being. I felt a sense of isolation and loneliness, as if I had lost my sense of belonging in the world. It was a difficult and challenging time as I grappled with a sense of loss and a deep longing to regain my independence and purpose.

Left with no choice, I returned to work for my ex-boss in Hollywood. The arrangement was peculiar - I didn't have to live with them, but I stayed two nights a week to take care of their children while she went out. It seemed somewhat fair to me, or so I thought.

Time flew by, and before we knew it, six months had passed since we became a couple. It was then, during all the chaos and uncertainty, that we decided to take the next step and get married. Scary? You say. Yes, it was devastating. Unfamiliar with what was going to happen next, I said, "YES!"

Chapter Thirteen
From Vows To Uncertainty: Navigating Early Marriage Challenges

When my partner and I decided to tie the knot, we chose to keep it a secret, sharing the moment only with two witnesses. Our wedding took place at the courthouse in Hollywood, and the simplicity of it all made me feel truly special.

As we exchanged vows in May 2014, little did I know that the marriage would unfold several difficult events in my life. In the beginning days of marriage, adjustments and challenges arose. We had to adapt to living together and merging our lives. Simple tasks like household chores required negotiation and compromise. Communication became vital to understand each other's expectations.

We learned to go through differences and find common ground. Financial responsibilities and decision-making were shared responsibilities. Balancing personal space and quality time became a delicate difficulty. Emotional support and understanding were crucial during this transition.

This marriage also led me to a heartwarming reunion with my family after six long years. When December came around, I made the journey to visit them, and to my surprise, it turned out to be an extraordinary gathering. There was no trace of fights or toxicity that had plagued previous family gatherings. Even my high school friends made an appearance, adding to the joyous atmosphere. It felt as if I had finally earned a place of importance within my family.

When my husband arrived to meet my family after some time of me being there alone, his friend from Estonia also joined us. We all slept in the same room, with his friend on the couch and us on the bed. Unfortunately, they had been drinking excessively, and my husband's behavior became irrational. He attempted to run away from the house despite the freezing cold and being in a foreign country. Thankfully, I managed to catch him before he reached the gate.

I guided him back to bed and tried to ensure his comfort. However, in his intoxicated state, he started making inappropriate advances toward me despite his friend being present in the same room. I firmly declined his advances, recognizing the inappropriateness of the situation. He reacted by threatening to leave me, calling me a horrible wife, and questioning the nature of our relationship. Internally, I felt scared, but I didn't let it show. I lied and said okay but requested to use the bathroom first. Instead, I stayed outside the room, waiting for him to fall asleep.

The next morning, I gathered the courage to confront my husband about the previous night's incident. However, he denied ever saying or doing anything inappropriate, dismissing my concerns. I chose to let it go, not because I imagined things but because I knew he wouldn't admit to his actions. We returned home together and resumed our work routines.

The excessive alcohol consumption and smoking had taken a toll on me, resulting in excruciating stomach acid issues. This discomfort pushed me to finally quit smoking cigarettes. As 2015 began, my biological clock started ticking louder. The desire to become a mother overwhelmed me, especially after visiting Poland and seeing how many of my high school friends were already married with children. I discussed my longing for motherhood with my husband and stopped taking birth control.

While he was aware of my decision, he didn't expect me to conceive so quickly. But to my luck, in April, I discovered that I was pregnant. Exhausted from his night shift at the hospital, I shared the news with my husband. His response was a simple "Okay" before he went to sleep.

Filled with a mix of excitement, happiness, and nervousness, I went to work, eager to share the news of my pregnancy. After finishing work, I returned home and sat down with my husband to discuss this significant milestone in our lives. To my shock and disbelief, he expressed that he believed we were too young to have children at just 30 years old. This statement caught me off guard, as we were already married, had a stable living situation in our paid-off apartment, and both held steady jobs.

I couldn't comprehend his perspective on age and parenthood. He even went as far as suggesting that I should go back to Poland or question the paternity of our child. It felt like a terrible nightmare that I desperately wished to wake up from. His hurtful words reached a new low when he added that he hoped I would have a miscarriage. My heart shattered, but I turned to prayer, placing my trust in God and surrendering to whatever destiny had in store for me and my unborn child.

Living in a disturbed and unhappy marriage took a toll on my emotional well-being. I felt trapped and suffocated, unable to express my true feelings. Every interaction left me feeling drained and emotionally exhausted. The constant tension and lack of connection left me feeling isolated. The absence of love and support created a deep sense of loneliness.

I yearned for affection and understanding that never seemed to come. Each day became a struggle as resentment and sadness consumed me. I began questioning my worth and wondered if happiness would ever find me.

The emotional torment felt unbearable, weighing heavily on my spirit. I longed for a way out, a chance to reclaim my happiness and peace. But despite the emotional torment, I refused to lose faith and continued to endure the challenges of my marriage.

The love and affection I had for my unborn baby served as a guiding light. I knew deep down that my child deserved a stable and loving family, even if it meant sacrificing my own happiness.

I held onto the hope that, in time, things would improve for the sake of our growing family. My determination to provide a nurturing environment for my child fueled my strength.

I was determined to provide a happy and loving place for my child so that he'll never have to bear the harsh cruelty of the world that I witnessed in my childhood.

With strong strength, I persevered, trusting that brighter days would eventually come. My commitment to creating a better future for my child kept me going, even in the darkest moments.

Weeks went by, and my husband accompanied me to the doctor for the first ultrasound. I was filled with anxiety, fearing that I might experience another miscarriage due to the cramps I was feeling.

Although he joined me, I knew he held onto the hope that the pregnancy wouldn't continue. However, as the ultrasound revealed a six-week-old baby with a strong, beating heart, my joy overwhelmed me.

In that moment, I even forgot about the fact that the baby's own father, my husband, didn't want this child. Despite his lack of interest, I confided in his mother, hoping for some support. To my surprise, she made two statements. First, she suggested that I leave the baby with her and go on my own. I firmly rejected that idea, as there was no way I could abandon my precious child.

Then, after a few seconds, she proposed that I stay with her son until the baby turned 18 years old. I couldn't understand the reasoning behind her conflicting statements. But soon, I decided to let the people talk and focus on my upcoming happiness, a piece of my soul – my baby!

As time passed, my belly grew larger, and I experienced constant and severe nausea. The discomfort was so intense that I lost 15 pounds because I couldn't eat much. Despite these challenges, I continued attending doctor appointments on my own, as my husband showed no interest in accompanying me.

Since I was a child, I had dreamed of becoming a mother and providing my children with the love and life experiences I had never received. Although I felt overwhelmed and unsure if I could handle everything on my own, the movements of my baby inside me filled me with hope for our future together and gave me the courage to move ahead with my life on my own!

Chapter Fourteen
Family Bonds: Turmoil, Forgiveness, And Redemption

In my quest for peace and a respite from the hustle and bustle of the world, I traveled to Poland, my ancestral land, in search of peace from my relatives. The fact that I had a secret inside me unknown to them all but my mother, who could not wait to see their reactions, which were unexpected, was amazing.

Stepping into my childhood house again, I felt the warmth engulfing me and love all around. The familiar aroma of homemade dumplings wafted through the air as laughter filled our living room. It was the perfect environment for what lay ahead.

I took time to plan carefully when to break the news about my pregnancy. Expectations became unbearable as minutes seemed like hours; however, I waited for a longer time period. As we sat together at dinner, exchanging stories and enjoying each other's company, it wasn't lost on me how everyone kept glancing at my surely growing stomach.

The moment was here. My heart pounding with excitement and fear, I rose up, brushing off any imaginary dust from myself. Expectant faces turned toward me, eyes fixed on me only as tenseness filled the atmosphere. "I have something special to share," I began with a trembling voice.

As I revealed the news that would completely change our lives, the room became still. "I am expecting a child," I stated, the words hanging in the air for some moments before they faded away. The atmosphere of the room was filled with collective gasps, followed by people's exclamations and laughter, intermingled with joyful tears staining their faces. This unexpected development caused both shock and happiness to sweep across everyone.

But in my great joy, I couldn't help overhearing some whispers about my size from behind me. How on earth does it happen that during pregnancy you can grow so big? They didn't know what they were saying because I had been eating healthily all along despite being pregnant. It did hurt a little, though, knowing how well I took care of myself not only physically but also mentally while carrying this baby inside me. However, love and excitement surrounded me.

On such lovely days like this one, when there was no storm in sight in their lives as yet, the whole family gathered outside their home. During the past week or so, my dad has been absorbed with vodka instead of food, as if that is what he eats and breaths every morning.

In a few days' time, his excessive drinking started bringing forth its consequences. Alcohol turned him into another person full of aggression and rage, but it felt like a switch being turned on, which brought chaos into our lives again.

My mother became the main object of my dad's fury amidst all these troubles. I had seen mind control and manipulation throughout my life, so I grew up being defensive of her. Therefore, I defended her again, just as I had done before to safeguard her from verbal abuse.

However, this only seemed to make the case worse. My father was overwhelmed by drunkenness, so he said some bitter words to me. This statement in which he insulted me with alcohol-stinking breaths will forever be entwined in my mind; "Your baby isn't worth shit." This minute reminded me of a knife piercing through my heart, for the pain was too much for me.

I felt numb and broken under his words' weight. How can a loving and tender-hearted father transform into callous and indifferent? The truth about our family was terrible to bear and it shattered all misconceptions.

In a fit of anger, my brother suddenly threw a punch at our father, hitting him squarely on his face. It hit hard like hell, while Dad reacted pretty fast. Then he jumped out of his chair both angry and drunk enough to grab axe in his hand. There is no danger more real than the one we were experiencing at that time.

We had a feeling that something was wrong so we ran toward our house, fumbling to secure the doors as fast as possible. The chaos filling our lives scared us; thus, panic raced through our veins. I turned and, with a tremor in my voice whispered to my mother, "We have to call the police. There must be a way out of this."

My mom however hesitated with an anxious tone, "What will people say?" This was where I knew society's judgement was the least of our concerns. "That doesn't matter," I replied resolutely, knowing that we would protect ourselves and put an end to this violence. "We need help....we need to call the police."

Summoning up all our bravery, we made a phone call that changed everything. At that moment, there seemed a ray of hope as they appeared in our lives, which were darkened by evil deeds. The law enforcement officers apprehended my father for what he had done, coming back on him at last; he would stay overnight in jail due to his self-destructive nature.

But then things took another turn that night. My dad, who was already weakened by addiction and evening's row, fell into a heart attack; it occurred to everyone how serious the matter was, so the authorities chose to move him to the hospital.

After the chaos and turmoil that had consumed my day, I desperately needed a moment of tranquillity. Seeking solace, therefore, I went to the doctor's office so as to get some solace from an ultrasound appointment. As I lay down on the examination table, my mind raced with worry and anxiety.
The doctor started the ultrasound by moving the wand gently over my stomach. Fear swept over me when he asked a question that sent shivers down my spine. "What do you know about your pregnancy?" he asked with a tone of concern.

My heart was pounding in my chest while I tried to gather myself together. "Everything has been going normally; I haven't had any problems yet," came tremblingly out of me. Despite this, there was still something within me that told me all is not well.

The doctor's face changed, and he spoke with both surprise and excitement in his voice. "But did they tell you that you are having twins?!" he exclaimed. For an instant, time stood still as those words echoed in my ears. My emotions were all over the place; it was so shocking, like being on a rollercoaster ride.

A mix of joy and fear overwhelmed me and brought tears streaming down my eyes. Those joyful tears ran down my cheeks, reflecting how much love I felt for these unexpected blessings. However, at the same time, I was also beset by a surge of apprehension, knowing that what lay ahead would be twice as difficult.

Unable to contain my excitement, I called my husband immediately because I couldn't hold back my excitement. He had been with his mom, and I could sense a glimmer of excitement in his voice for the first time. The thought of our growing family filled my heart with hope and anticipation.

A mix of joy and amazement hung in the air as news spread throughout our extended family. The sudden discovery of twins brought an extra level to our journey that would require more strength, support and love.

The next day, I gathered some courage and suggested visiting Dad at the hospital. For her part my mother hesitated thinking it was a lunatic idea, but I insisted, telling her that this might be his turning point when he needed us most.

When we entered my father's room, shock was evident on his face. Tears welled up in his eyes as soon as he realized that I had come to see him. He begged for forgiveness, full of remorse in his voice. That very moment something shifted within me tears streaming down my face escaping from deep within me. It was a profound and emotional conversation between father and daughter.

That day was a significant turning point in my father's life. He swore to himself and to us that he would never touch alcohol again... And true to his word, he kept firm to it all throughout.

My dad's transformation taught me a valuable lesson – it's never too late to change, to become a better version of oneself. Witnessing his journey of redemption filled me with hope and a renewed belief in the power of love, forgiveness, and personal growth.

From then on, our relationship with my dad took a different course. We had to rebuild trust, heal each other and understand this new situation we were in. From that point on, we became a single family unit supporting one another through the good times and bad times of life.

My father was struggling with his alcohol addiction to show us that even when in the darkest moments of our lives, we can still redeem ourselves by rewriting our stories so as not to ever become hopeless cases. It proved how strong humans can be in spirit and how love can bring miracles.

And so, as we moved forward together, I held onto the profound lesson my dad taught me - that it's never too late to change, to mend broken relationships, and to become the best version of ourselves.

Chapter Fifteen
A Mother's Struggle: Coping With Pregnancy Complications

As I returned to the USA from my visit to Poland, life gradually settled back into its usual routine of work and being a wife. However, on one fateful day, when my husband was enjoying a sound sleep after his night shift at the hospital, I found myself falling ill.

It started suddenly with me experiencing severe nausea. It was unending and scary because I was already in my 23rd week of pregnancy. My instincts told me that something terrible had occurred. For even worse luck, diarrhea also struck me at this time.

Realizing the urgency of the situation, I shook my husband awake and urgently told him that we needed to go to the emergency room.

Unfortunately, it took us a long while for him to find parking instead of just dropping me off at the emergency entrance. As we were driving, I suddenly felt extreme nausea, which made me vomit right there in the car. Luckily, I had a plastic bag that contained most of it, but not without leaving behind traces on my trousers which no doubt resulted in soiling my pants. Yes! I pooped in my pants!!!

Upon arrival at the hospital, they directed me to sit in a wheelchair as we could go up to the delivery floor. But I was determined to walk by myself. To my dismay, the attendant insisted that I sit down, claiming that unless I did so, he/she would not let me pass through the door. Embarrassed, I tried to express quietly that I had messed up myself and did not wish to make the seat messy. The ticketing clerk assured me that they always cleaned the seats; thus, I took a seat, grudgingly aware of my uncomfortable situation.

The pungent smell stayed with us until we went up to the delivery floor, making me acutely self-conscious. I refused to sit upright in my soiled pants throughout the journey. On arrival, there was no available bed for me to be taken into it. They put me in a waiting room that made it obvious pregnant women were expecting their babies any time soon, for other expectant parents were sitting around smiling at each other. For my part, I felt infinitely out of place and mortified while seated in ruined underwear.

I, therefore, approached one of the nurses with a plea for one of those covers that leave your butts partially exposed during the examination as per normal practices observed by patients when being treated in hospitals. My request was made politely hoping she would appreciate the urgency of my case. On her part, she insisted that a bed should first be available before issuing anything else to patients; however, she told me to wait until then. Nonetheless, she continued asking me to just give her time as well.

I was irritated by her reaction, and so I managed to summon some courage to say something once more, this time with a little of anger in my voice. I shouted out loudly, "Please just let me have it! Haven't you noticed? I pooped on myself!" Her eyes were opened wide by my statement; afterward she gave in. "Oh my goodness, okay," said she, "Here you go. Get two covers plus wipes."

After spending four agonizing hours because of food poisoning, I got an IV to rebuild my system and keep my twins and myself hydrated. The dehydration was so bad that at 23 weeks of being pregnant, it even caused contractions. It was such a stressful time.

Back at home, casually laughing, my mother-in-law mentioned off-handedly, "Oh, I forgot to tell you I left the spring rolls in the fridge this morning and forgot to put them away last night." At that particular moment, as if I could kill her with the look on my eyes a surge of anger and frustration ran through me. Who does anything like that?

For several days that followed, I couldn't bear looking at her face straight into her eyes as well as emotions welled up inside me. Resentment remained but with time passed slowly, and I learned how to walk away from what happened.

I was compelled to make the difficult decision to quit my job at 28 weeks into my pregnancy as time flew by. I just couldn't go on any more because the doctor advised me to take it easy. Carrying twins had taken a toll on my body, leaving me completely worn out.

Unfortunately, my journey toward motherhood didn't go as planned. At 33 weeks of pregnancy, the contractions started and couldn't be stopped by doctors. Panic-stricken, I reached out to everyone back home in our country, asking them to pray for my babies. The next morning's C-section could only be successful with someone's support.

In a moment of vulnerability, I called my mom, hoping for comfort and reassurance. But she picked up her phone while she was at work, where she serves as an elementary school teacher. Totally overcome with emotions, I wept and bared my soul, but she just said, "I can't talk now; I am in class", then hung up abruptly.

My heart broke into pieces. My husband, too, was right there on a chair near me, sleeping due to his own exhaustion, thus causing an overwhelming sense of loneliness that came over me. It was beyond belief that in such a crucial time as this one my own mother could not spare some minutes for me.

I wept all night, pleading with God that my babies would be born alive; this was the only thing I wanted again these years since then. On the following morning, at thirty-three weeks gestation, my beautiful little ones arrived into this world.

But to my distress, this beautiful moment became a point of concern. My daughter did not breathe and hence had to be resuscitated by medics while my son went straight into an incubator where he took his first breath but with the help of machines placed inside him too. As they were taken away from me quickly to the NICU (Neonatal Intensive Care Unit), the recovery room awaited news of anxiety.

My baby was born at 10:30 am and the next morning, my husband left to attend a marathon in another state. I wanted him to stay with me, but he insisted that his trip was his dream and that he had to stay for his team. Finally, I agreed without much enthusiasm, knowing that the nurses were there for mothers' welfare. However, deep inside me, I hoped that he would decide to remain with us realizing how vulnerable we still were.

Sitting in the hospital bed, worried and anxious about the life ahead of me, it occurred to me what kind of childhood I hoped for my kids. I wished that when they grew up, they never experienced things like I did; instead, they should be nurtured in an environment where everyone has some form of assistance, unlike what happened to me during my parenthood days.

I didn't want to recreate some things from my own childhood while raising my children. But feeling invisible and neglected as a child, helped me understand how important it is to listen to what my children say wholeheartedly. Their point of view still counts forevermore and it's time I let them know that if they ever require any help or guidance, then Mum will be there for them.

Again, I have learned that expressing emotions and validating them is also crucial. Allowing my kids to express themselves freely has always been my dream so that they could understand that human being can experience the full spectrum of emotions. The most important thing was to create a safe environment for them where they could build their emotional strength and intelligence.

Moreover, while developing my parenting models, I wanted them to be characterized by predictability and stability. I wished for my children to grow up knowing that our home would always be there in all situations. This implied having routines, limitations, and a predictable framework which were areas of reliance.

However, all said and done, love, respect and kindness were some of the qualities I desired in such an environment. My partner and I wanted to have a nurturing family relationship therefore, it was necessary that we live by these values on a daily basis. It was never easy, as it required continuous thinking about it as well as growth, but this journey was for the happiness of my own children.

Being in the middle of uncertainty and problems that come with premature births has made me understand how important a strong support system is. It was difficult for me to stand my husband's absence during that critical moment, but I got strength from inside that helped me be there for my children. Determined to give them the sanctuary they deserved, I held on to them tight and loved them unconditionally.

And so, this journey continued toward creating a nurturing, supportive family. It presented new opportunities to learn and grow each day while giving my children a loving environment.

My vision was to create a warm childhood characterized by understanding and steady-flowing love for my children. I remained full of hope as I set out knowing one day they would recall their upbringing with nostalgia, aware that their family surrounded them with love from birth till now. This was my wish!

Chapter Sixteen
In The Shadow Of The Nicu: Trials Of Motherhood

After three long days in the hospital, I finally got to go home. It was a bittersweet moment as I left without my precious babies. My ex-boss unexpectedly offered to give me a ride home. It was a kind gesture, but it only served as a painful reminder of the life I had before everything changed.

As I walked through the door of my empty home, my heart shattered into a million pieces. The silence echoed in the empty rooms, increasing the emptiness I felt inside. It was a stark contrast to the chaotic and uncertain environment I had become accustomed to in the NICU.

Those days spent in the NICU were a rollercoaster of emotions. Every minute, every second, I was taught the value of faith, patience, and never giving up. My fragile little ones were fighting for their lives, and I had to summon every ounce of strength within me to be their pillar of support.

I spent endless hours in the hospital, tending to their every need. From changing their tiny diapers to feeding them, I did everything I could to ensure their well-being. The days blurred together as I tirelessly cared for them, my exhaustion creeping in like a heavy fog.

The toll on my body was evident. My legs swelled up to the point where even the nurses grew concerned. They urged me to rest, offering me a place to lie down beside the NICU beds. It was a heartbreaking decision, torn between wanting to be by my babies' side every waking moment and acknowledging the importance of taking care of myself.

In that moment, I realized the immense strength and sacrifice that motherhood demands. It was a journey that tested not only my physical endurance but also my emotional fortitude. The love I felt for my children was overwhelming, propelling me forward even when I felt like crumbling under the weight of uncertainty.

As I lay beside their NICU beds, I whispered words of encouragement and love into the sterile air. I prayed for their strength and resilience, willing them to fight with every fiber of their being. And though the road ahead was uncertain, I vowed to be their strong source of love and support.

In the midst of the pain and heartache, I found peace in knowing that these trying moments were shaping me into a stronger person. The NICU became my classroom, teaching me the true meaning of strength, hope, and the unbreakable bond between a mother and her children.

So, with a heavy heart, I sat in my empty home, aching for the presence of my babies. But I knew that, for now, the NICU was where they needed to be. And I would continue to be their pillar of strength, holding onto the belief that one day soon, we would all be reunited, forever changed by the journey we had endured together.

The weight of motherhood guilt bore down on me relentlessly. My heart ached as I watched my precious babies fight for their lives, struggling just to take each breath. It was a stark reminder of how easily we take the simple act of breathing for granted. My babies relied on a CPAP machine to help them breathe, a constant reminder of their fragile state.

In the depths of my soul, I carried the burden of this difficult time. My husband caught up in the demands of work and school, was rarely present at the hospital. He would often tell me, "My training is crucial, and school needs my results." While I understood the importance of his commitments, it pained me that he couldn't be there more often for our children during this critical period.

The moment I received the news about my son's brain bleeds, terror gripped every fiber of my being. I was overwhelmed with fear and uncertainty. I immediately called my husband, desperately urging him to come to the hospital. To my disbelief, he casually replied, "I'm going for a run right now. I told you I need to work out. I'll come by for a little while when I'm done." The coldness in his response pierced my heart as I struggled to comprehend how someone could be so detached from their own flesh and blood. In that moment, I realized that it was just me and my babies facing life and all its hardships alone.

The emotional trauma I experienced was indescribable. Motherhood came with an overwhelming sense of responsibility and a fierce protective instinct that only grew stronger in the face of adversity. My love for my children knew no bounds, and it was devastating to witness their struggles while feeling the absence of their father's support.

Yet, during all the struggles, I found strength within myself. The bond between me and my babies grew stronger with each passing day as I remained determined to provide them with the best possible care.

Though the weight of motherhood guilt still lingered, I drew comfort from the unbreakable connection I shared with my children. They became my driving force, reminding me of the incredible love that exists within a mother's heart.

Just a week before my twins were supposed to come home, a devastating incident occurred. A pipe in the babies' room at our house suddenly burst, causing extensive flooding. The room was completely destroyed, and mold began to grow rapidly. The thought of bringing my fragile babies to such a ruined environment was heartbreaking.

I fought tirelessly with our house insurance company, desperately pleading with them to understand the urgency and devastation we were facing. After a long and exhausting battle, they finally agreed to cover our stay in a hotel while our home underwent renovation.

The emotions I experienced were overwhelming. Alongside the joy and anticipation of bringing my babies home, there was a deep pain in realizing that our once peaceful and safe haven had turned into a place of chaos and destruction. It served as a stark reminder of how quickly life can change and how fragile our surroundings can be.

However, I refused to let despair consume me. I drew strength from the determination that had carried me thus far. I understood that my babies needed a safe and nurturing environment to continue their recovery journey. So, I embraced the challenges, fought for what was right, and sought temporary refuge for my family.

Although the road ahead still seemed uncertain, I held onto the belief that we would overcome this setback just as we had overcome numerous other obstacles. My love for my babies became the driving force that propelled me forward, reminding me that I would do whatever it took to provide them with the care and comfort they deserved.

It was a heartbreaking moment when we couldn't bring our babies home for Christmas. Their first holiday was spent in a hotel room, and I couldn't help but feel a deep sense of sadness and loneliness. My emotions were overwhelming, and the exhaustion was taking its toll on me. Despite it all, I tried to stay positive and remind myself that my babies were alive and thriving.

After six long weeks, we finally returned home. It was a moment of relief and joy, a fresh start for our family. The next day, my husband and I decided to take a walk in the park. Little did I know that a devastating discovery awaited me. As my husband showed me something on his phone, a text message from another woman appeared. My heart sank as I read their explicit conversation - they were engaging in sexual messaging. What made it worse was that he had even sent her pictures of himself posing provocatively in front of a mirror.

The pain was unbearable. I couldn't understand how he could betray me like this, especially during such a challenging time in our lives. I was only three months postpartum after giving premature birth, dealing with depression, overwhelming stress, and a deep sense of loneliness. And yet, he had the audacity to be upset with me because I couldn't fulfill his sexual desires. It felt like a dagger through my already shattered heart.

I confronted the woman he was having an explicit conversation with, and she dared to blame him for allowing me to touch his phone. She advised him to change the password, and he did without hesitation. I couldn't believe what I was hearing and witnessing. It shattered my trust even further.

Despite the pain and betrayal, I felt trapped. I didn't have a job, and the fear of starting over on my own kept me from leaving. I stayed, pretending like nothing had happened, burying my emotions deep within me.

After six months, I found it in my heart to forgive my mother. I wanted her to be a part of my children's lives, so I shared pictures of them with her and we began to rebuild our relationship. I invited her and my father to visit us to meet their precious grandchildren. They accepted and came to visit us during the summer.

However, even during their visit, I was still struggling with postpartum depression, a condition I wasn't even aware of at the time. It was a constant internal battle, fighting against my own thoughts and emotions. The weight of it all was overwhelming.

I remember standing in the kitchen, overwhelmed with emotions, and I confided in my mother. I told her that sometimes I felt so overwhelmed that I didn't want to be a mother. It saddened me even to think that way, but I didn't know how to process those feelings. Instead of understanding or offering support, my mother looked at me with anger in her eyes and spoke sharply, saying, "How can you even say that!? You're an awful mother for thinking such things!" Then, she walked away. The weight of guilt consumed me, but I was determined to be the best mother I could be, showing my babies the love that I had always longed for.

After the summer, my parents went back home, and my husband's friends came to visit him. They went out, leaving me at home with the babies. When my husband returned, he was heavily intoxicated and began behaving recklessly. Despite my pleas, he insisted on having sex and became aggressive when I refused, disregarding the fact that our babies were sleeping. He started to hurl insults at me, calling me useless, and then he broke down into tears, his drunken ramblings becoming more nonsensical.

At one point, he even attempted to take the car keys, intending to drive in his intoxicated state. I stood my ground, refusing to let him endanger himself or others. In response, he became even more volatile, throwing things around the house, and I began to fear for my safety.

In desperation, I called his mother and gave her an ultimatum: *she had ten minutes to come and take her son, or I would involve the authorities.* She arrived and took him to her place, his drunken state making it difficult for him to comprehend the seriousness of his actions. The next morning, he acted as if nothing had happened, offering no apologies or acknowledgment of the chaos he had caused. It was as if that night didn't even exist in his mind.

His casual and carefree behavior in the aftermath of that chaotic night only intensified my feelings of frustration and hurt. It was incredibly difficult for me to comprehend how he could simply brush off the severity of his actions and the impact they had on our relationship and family.

I felt a deep sense of betrayal as I questioned whether I had made the right choice in building a life with someone who could so easily disregard my emotions and the well-being of our children. One thing I knew for sure was that the wounds from that night and the emotional toll it took on me would take a significant amount of time to heal, if they could ever fully mend at all.

Chapter Seventeen
Navigating Nightmares: A Tale Of Stange Happenings

While I was in the early stages of my pregnancy with twins, we made the decision to purchase a house. It was the year 2015, and the house had been on the market for over three years. Something about the house gave me a sense of unease, but unfortunately, the realtor we hired happened to be a friend's mother. She was more interested in making a profit than considering our concerns.

Little did I know that the broken pipe we had to deal with after the twins were born would be the least of our worries. The true troubles lay in the things that unfolded within those walls, things that I couldn't fully understand as they were happening. It was a distressing and confusing time, filled with moments that left me feeling overwhelmed and helpless. The weight of the situation only grew as I struggled to make sense of our decisions and the consequences we were facing in our new home.

After the twins were born, strange occurrences began happening in our home. At first, I brushed them off, believing that it was simply the exhaustion of caring for two infants on my own that was playing tricks on my mind. Night after night, I found myself trapped in the same recurring nightmare. I ignored it as the result of my sleep-deprived state, desperately hoping that it would fade away.

But then, one fateful night, while my husband slept beside me, his mumbling in his sleep grew louder and more intense. I couldn't comprehend his words, as if someone was forcefully silencing him. Startled, I woke him up, and his eyes widened with terror as he blurted out, "Oh my God! I was screaming for you to wake me up!"

Confused, I explained that I hadn't heard any clear cries for help, only muffled mumbling. I couldn't ignore the eerie coincidence when he revealed the details of his nightmare—a haunting old lady dressed in black, preventing him from entering our own house, choking him in his dream. My heart sank, my jaw dropping in disbelief. How could he describe the exact same old lady that had been haunting me night after night?

An unsettling feeling washed over me as we exchanged our experiences. He tried to mask his fear, unwilling to show any vulnerability, and returned to sleep. But for me, the fear lingered, intensifying my sense of unease. It was clear that something beyond our comprehension was happening, and I couldn't help but wonder what dreadful secrets our new home held.

As I drifted off to sleep, the presence of that haunting old lady returned, tormenting me once again. Fear gripped my heart as I mustered the courage to confront her in my nightmare. "What do you want?" I demanded, my voice trembling. To my horror, she pointed directly at my precious baby son. The mere thought of harm coming to him sent shivers down my spine, and I abruptly woke up, my entire being consumed by fear.

Determined to protect my family, I approached my husband and insisted that it was time to leave this house of terrible memories behind. I couldn't bear to stay any longer; the weight of these haunting experiences had become unbearable. But he dismissed my concerns, accusing me of overreacting. Little did he know that these strange occurrences were taking a toll on my sanity.

Yet, the strange happenings continued, intensifying my fears. A bad smell of rotten onions polluted the air whenever I was near my son, but only within the confines of our home. The odor was overpowering, making me gag and wince with disgust. It was as if an unseen force was trying to communicate with me, using this foul scent to send a chilling message.

The weight of these experiences and the overwhelming sense of danger grew with each passing day. Deep down, I knew something was terribly wrong with this house, and I couldn't bear to subject my family to its sinister presence any longer.

One day, I decided to invite my friend and her two adorable babies over for a casual get-together at our house. As we sat around the table and on the couch, engrossed in conversation, the unexpected occurred. We witnessed objects moving on their own accord. I know it sounds unbelievable, but it happened right before our eyes!

My friend had a can of coke placed on the table, and to our shock, it began to rotate on its own, not just sliding from side to side, but actually spinning in a complete circle, as if it had a mind of its own. The fear in my friend's eyes mirrored my own terror, and she exclaimed, "Did you see that?!" I could only nod in disbelief, confirming that I, too, had witnessed this inexplicable phenomenon. The can spun once again, defying all rational explanations.

In that moment, fear took hold of us, and my friend hastily gathered her children, leaving the house in a hurry. Feeling a surge of panic and anxiety, I swiftly took my own kids to the car and went to the park, hoping that the fresh air and open space would calm my troubled mind. But the incident had only added to the overwhelming anxiety and fear that already weighed heavily on my shoulders.

After enduring the terrifying experiences in our previous house, I desperately pleaded with my husband to consider moving. Finally, after much persuasion and discussion, he agreed! Oh, what a relief! We embarked on a search for a new home, hoping to find a place that would bring us peace and happiness. And guess what? Our prayers were answered when we stumbled upon a dream house in Port Saint Lucie, Florida.

It was everything we had ever envisioned—a spacious house with an expansive half-acre yard, complete with a delightful pool for the kids to enjoy. And the best part? No trace of that dreadful rotten onion smell! We couldn't contain our excitement; it felt like destiny had led us to this perfect abode, a sanctuary where we could build a lifetime of beautiful memories. So, with our twins still just a year and a half old, we made the decision to move and embark on a new chapter of our lives in this idyllic home.

Despite my husband securing a job at a hospital in our new city, he couldn't help but constantly complain about the pay cut he had to endure compared to his previous well-paid position. I tried my best to explain to him that money shouldn't be the sole measure of our happiness. Our new home offered us a sense of tranquility and peace that was priceless. But no matter how much I emphasized this, he remained miserable, always prioritizing money above all else.

As time went by, hurricane season approached, bringing with it the looming threat of a category 5 hurricane that was projected to destroy the entire state of Florida. Concerned for our safety, I urged my husband to consider driving north for a few days until the storm passed. However, he dismissed my concerns, accusing me of overreacting. I suggested covering our windows with plywood as a precautionary measure, but he adamantly refused.

Feeling helpless and desperate, I turned to my friends on Facebook, reaching out for assistance in acquiring some plywood to secure our windows. To my surprise, they couldn't comprehend why my husband would willingly put our family at risk by disregarding the imminent danger that the hurricane posed to our region. It was a difficult and frustrating situation as I struggled to navigate my husband's stubbornness in the face of such potential danger.

I was filled with fear and panic as I realized that the noise I heard was actually a sign of an approaching tornado. I rushed back inside, my heart pounding, and urged my husband to take cover with me and the kids. He finally understood the severity of the situation and we huddled together, praying for our safety. The wind howled outside, rain poured relentlessly, and I couldn't help but think about the fragility of our new home and the safety of our family.

The day when a tornado was predicted, to our luck, it slowed down. But to my anxious mind, I decided to go out and see if everything was all right. The minute I stepped out, I heard a loud noise of an airplane passing by. Alarmed by the situation, I went inside and Googled it. To my surprise, it meant that whenever one hears an airplane engine sound during the hurricane season, it means a tornado is close by.

Knowing this truth, my anxiety skyrocketed, reaching levels I had never experienced before. I immediately took my children to their room, ensuring the closet was open and the mattress was ready to shield us if needed. My husband, however, dismissed my concerns with laughter, accusing me of overreacting as usual.

But the very next day, we saw the news report confirming that a tornado had touched down just half a mile away from our home. In that moment, I vowed to myself that I would never again ignore my instincts when it came to the safety of our children. I made a promise that the next time a hurricane threatened our area, I would take the kids and drive away to a safer location.

Thankfully, the tornado passed without causing any major damage to our neighborhood, but the experience left us shaken. It was a wake-up call for both of us, reminding us of the importance of being prepared and prioritizing the safety of our loved ones over anything else.

Living through that hurricane season was a turning point for us. It made us realize the value of our new home, not just in terms of physical comfort but also in terms of the peace and security it brought to our lives. We were grateful for our fresh start in Port Saint Lucie, and we were determined to build a happy and safe life for our family in our new surroundings.

After the end of hurricane season, it was time to shift our focus toward a happier occasion—the second birthday of our twins! I couldn't contain my excitement as I meticulously planned every detail of the celebration a whole month in advance. From the decorations to the food and even a bounce house, I poured my heart and soul into creating the perfect birthday party for them.

It was a joyous occasion that held a special significance for me—it was not only about celebrating their milestones but also about healing my own inner child. I felt immensely blessed to be able to give them the kind of birthday party that I had always dreamed of as a child. Even though they might not remember it, I knew that I would cherish these memories and the love-filled atmosphere of their birthday party for years to come.

Living with my husband had become a constant battle. No matter how hard I tried, it seemed like nothing was ever good enough for him. His dissatisfaction with his job consumed him, and he took it out on me. He belittled me for not working and for relying on his income. He criticized my appearance, making me feel inadequate and unworthy. Despite all my efforts to support him and take care of our children and our home, it was never enough to earn his respect or appreciation.

His verbal attacks on my self-esteem were bad enough, but it didn't stop there. He would throw tantrums, breaking things and creating an atmosphere of fear and tension in our home. I began to fear for my safety and the safety of our children. It was a living nightmare.

I felt trapped and scared. I constantly walked on eggshells, trying to avoid triggering his anger. It was as if I had lost my voice and my autonomy. I had become a puppet, always doing whatever he demanded, just to keep the peace and avoid further conflict.

I knew deep down that this was not a healthy or loving relationship. I deserved better, and so did my children. It was time for me to find the strength to break free from this cycle of abuse and create a safe and loving environment for myself and my kids.

I felt devastated when my husband made the decision to apply for a job in Los Angeles without even discussing it with me. I expressed my concerns, telling him that I didn't want to leave Florida, but he seemed determined to pursue his dream of living in California. The thought of staying behind without him filled me with fear and insecurity. My self-esteem had been shattered by his constant criticism about my weight and the belief that I couldn't survive financially on my own with two children. I felt trapped and believed that no one else would want me in my current state.

Despite my reservations, I reluctantly started packing our belongings, feeling a mix of sadness and resignation. I even helped him move one of our cars to Los Angeles despite my own doubts and fears about the future.

With my parents graciously offering to stay with the twins, we embarked on a grueling 38-hour drive to Los Angeles. It was a marathon of non-stop driving, only pausing for necessary gas stops. My husband had to start his new job earlier, so I returned home alone, facing the daunting task of selling our furniture and car and finding someone to rent our house.

The weight of responsibility pressed heavily on my shoulders as I navigated the challenges of being a single parent to two-and-a-half-year-old twins. The constant fear of being alone intensified during those six weeks as I tackled the overwhelming to-do list while trying to keep my own emotions in check.

Adding to my already mounting fears, my alarm suddenly went off one terrifying night, indicating that the garage door was open. Panic consumed me as I immediately dialed the police for help. The voice on the other end of the line told me to wait for them, but it felt like an eternity as I anxiously awaited their arrival.

Finally, after 15 agonizing minutes, they showed up at my doorstep. Can you imagine? I couldn't believe it. They casually mentioned that it could have been a simple alarm mistake, something that apparently happens often.

Then, shockingly, they asked if I had gone into the garage to check. I was appalled by their suggestion. Why on earth would I risk my safety and go inside to investigate? I was here alone with my two young children, and they expected me to be the one to confront any potential danger. It was absolutely ridiculous. I was furious. Not only did they take their sweet time getting here, but now they were asking me to put myself at risk.

The officer tried to calm me down, explaining that they found the door open, but whoever had triggered the alarm had fled. Sleep eluded me after that incident. I immediately called my husband, hoping for some reassurance, some comfort. But his response was dismissive, telling me I was probably overreacting. I felt utterly hopeless. All I wanted was someone to embrace me, to tell me everything would be okay.

Feeling overwhelmed and desperate for support, I made the difficult decision to sell all of our belongings as quickly as possible. I needed to find a place to stay with my mother-in-law, just so I wouldn't have to be alone anymore. It was a daunting task, but I took it upon myself to handle everything.

However, my husband dismissed my efforts, telling me it wasn't a big deal and that anyone could do it. It hurt deeply that I never received any acknowledgment or appreciation from him. It was like hearing my own mother's critical voice, but I had learned to ignore these red flags in people's behavior.

Living in a house devoid of emotions only served to mask these warning signs. We ended up staying in that house for just a year and a half, despite my initial belief that it would be our forever home.

Eventually, we moved to Los Angeles County, settling at a military base in San Pedro. The hope of a fresh start and a supportive community kept me going, even though I still carried the weight of my past experiences.

Chapter Eighteen
Love, Sacrifice, And Community: Life On The Military Base

We made the decision to relocate to San Pedro, California, a place I had never been before. It was a significant move for us, as my husband was a soldier in the reserves and we were moving to a military base. The idea of living on a military base was new to me, but I was excited for the adventure that awaited us.

As we settled into our new home, I quickly realized that this environment offered a level of safety and security that I had never experienced before. With my husband being a soldier, there was a sense of protection that surrounded us. I could finally take a seat on a park bench by the playground and watch my children run around without the constant fear of someone trying to harm them. The weight of anxiety that had plagued me for so long began to ease, and I could breathe a little easier.

Living on the military base also introduced me to a whole new community - the military wives. It was a revelation to me how underappreciated these incredible women were. They were the backbone of their families, constantly uprooting their lives every few years to follow their husbands' military assignments. They were the ones who held everything together while their husbands were away, juggling the responsibilities of raising children, managing households, and dealing with the emotional toll of separation.

I soon found myself surrounded by these amazing women who, like me, were mostly stay-at-home moms. We formed a tight-knit group, supporting and leaning on one another through the ups and downs of military life. We shared stories, laughter, and tears, finding peace in the fact that we were not alone in our struggles and triumphs.

In the midst of our conversations, I couldn't help but be in awe of the strength and resilience these women possessed. They faced constant change, adapting to new surroundings, making new friends, and saying goodbye when the time came to move again. Their lives were a constant juggle between packing, unpacking, and starting over. Yet, despite the challenges, they remained steadfast and committed to their families and their husbands' service to the country.

Living on the military base in San Pedro, California, opened my eyes to a world I had never known. It was a place where safety and peace of mind were a reality, where military wives were the unsung heroes, and where a community of strong, supportive women thrived. And in this newfound environment, I found the strength to face my fears and embrace the uncertainties that military life brought.

Regardless of their personal preferences, military families have to go wherever the military orders take them. It's a sacrifice that the soldiers make for the service, but let's not forget about their wives. These women provide immense support and face numerous challenges in constantly moving with their families. It made me appreciate my own situation, as while my husband and I moved frequently, we had the luxury of choosing our destinations. However, military families don't have that option. They must go wherever they are told.

On the other side, my husband had committed himself to working at the VA clinic in West Beverly Hills, which was his dream job. However, if I'm being honest, a significant factor in his decision was the dream benefits that came with the job. He had to endure a grueling commute of 30 miles each way, which, in the notorious Los Angeles traffic, translated to a two-hour journey one way.

Every day, my husband would come home to a warm meal, waiting on the table for the kids. They would already be bathed and everyone would be in a state of relaxation. As a stay-at-home mom and wife, my main role was to take care of the household. I had become accustomed to cooking only Asian food, as my husband insisted on it and would argue if I made anything else. So, I would prepare separate dinners for the kids and him, making sure to cater to his preferences.

I took pride in being a devoted wife and mother, always ensuring that my husband had breakfast ready, packed lunch for work, and a delicious dinner waiting for him when he returned home. I would even wash and scrub his work clothes, setting them aside for him to wear. It was my way of showing him love and appreciation.

We were both striving to find happiness in our new life in San Pedro. I held onto the hope that my husband's dream job would bring us the peace and contentment we had been seeking.

As time went on, my husband and I began to complain about his long commute and how his job at the clinic wasn't fulfilling compared to his previous work at the hospital. The dissatisfaction started to create a distance between us. It became a regular part of my life to rely on wine in order to feel intimate with my own husband. He would express his frustration about it, but I would dismiss it as my own insecurities when, in reality, it was he who seemed distant.

I struggled to find my place in California. I felt lonely, and the weather wasn't as pleasant as he had promised. Our neighbors were noisy at night, making it difficult for me to sleep well.

One day, our daughter fell ill while my husband was on his way to work. I called him in a panic, pleading for him to come home and help me take her to the pediatrician. I asked him to stay with our son while I took care of our sick daughter. His response shocked me: "My team at the clinic needs me. I can't take off for this nonsense."

In desperation, I threatened him with divorce, hoping it would make him realize the gravity of the situation. He finally came home, but I couldn't believe that he would prioritize the needs of strangers over his own family.

As my depression began to take hold, my husband suggested that I try using marijuana, which was legal in California. Desperate for any relief, I started using it, finding that it helped me cope with the challenges in my relationship. It was as if all the warning signs and red flags turned into green lights. I would only smoke when the kids were asleep and my husband was home, always making sure he was there in case of any emergencies.

After some time, we decided to take a weekend trip to San Diego. The moment we set foot in the city, we fell in love with its peaceful and serene atmosphere. It was a stark contrast to the bustling streets of Los Angeles.

Touched by this beautiful place, we made the decision to move there, hoping that this change would bring the happiness and peace we had been seeking. My husband was finally able to secure a job in a hospital, which had always been his dream. I believed that this new opportunity would bring fulfillment and harmony to our lives.

To make the transition smoother, we invited my parents to stay with us for six months and assist us with the move. During this time, a friend from Poland came to visit us. My mother, always seeking attention, indulged in some drinks with my friend.

Though I refrained from drinking that day, I couldn't help but notice the changes in my mother's behavior. She seemed determined to assert her dominance and fulfill her own desires, regardless of the impact on others.

It was during this gathering that she revealed her intention to visit the Grand Canyon, claiming it was her dream, but I couldn't shake the feeling that her true motive was to one-up a friend. The audacity and selfishness of her statement left me stunned. I silently resolved that I would not be taking her to the Grand Canyon, as it felt morally wrong to indulge her manipulative desires.

This incident served as a turning point, allowing me to see my mother's true colors. The veil of manipulation that she had once created around me began to dissolve, revealing the red flags that had always been present. It troubled me deeply, but I chose to focus on the future ahead, on the promise of a better life in the vibrant city of San Diego.

As we settled into our new home in San Diego, I couldn't help but feel a sense of hope for a brighter future. Wanting to treat myself and perhaps seek some validation, I convinced my husband to agree to buy a new car for me. He had his work car, and I had a large SUV that I didn't really need. I had my sights set on a small, luxurious car, a BMW Series 7, which was my dream car. However, my husband wasn't enthusiastic about the idea and didn't share the same passion for cars that I did.

In an effort to compromise, he surprised me with a BMW convertible, similar to the one he had when we first met, albeit an older model. While it wasn't exactly the car of my dreams, it made him happy, and I was grateful for the gesture. We found a used one that I fell in love with, and I brought it home with excitement.

But as soon as my mother laid eyes on it, she began to criticize. She questioned why I needed a third car and why it was so small, and she expressed her dislike for the dark blue color. She even went on to critique our new house, suggesting that the kitchen should be painted a lighter color and that the house itself was too big. Her constant complaints and demands for perfection started to wear on me, making me question my choices and desires.

Despite my mother's negativity, I held onto my gratitude for the opportunities and blessings that had come our way. I knew deep down that it was important to focus on the positive aspects of our new life in San Diego rather than getting caught up in the opinions of others.

During the COVID-19 pandemic, our household fell victim to the virus. It started with my husband, who developed a high fever and felt completely drained, sleeping for almost half a day.

Soon after, my parents and children also began experiencing fevers and fatigue. As for me, I, too, succumbed to the illness, but the challenge was that I had to continue tending to my family's needs while being sick myself. It was a difficult time, but we supported each other as best we could.

During my sickness, I noticed that my husband struggled to believe the severity of my symptoms. He would often dismiss my illness as mere exaggeration, urging me to stop overreacting.

Frustrated by his lack of empathy, I found myself expressing the desire to pay him for his kindness and assistance, similar to how he received payment for his work at the hospital. As the days dragged on in lockdown, with my mother and I confined together, I turned to marijuana as a coping mechanism. It helped me muster the courage to engage in intimacy with my husband, a healthier alternative to relying on alcohol to numb myself during those moments. It puzzled me how he never questioned why I felt the need to be intoxicated to be intimate with him, yet he would complain about it happening too frequently.

One day, I discovered that I was pregnant again. Even before taking a test, I could feel the familiar surge of hormones coursing through my body, just like when I was pregnant with my twins.

In that moment, I couldn't help but wonder if my husband had gotten me pregnant because we were slowly drifting apart, becoming more like roommates than a married couple. Our affection for one another had dwindled, and I found myself fulfilling my role as a wife by taking care of household chores, cooking, and looking after our children. I was filled with fear as thoughts raced through my mind. I prayed, hoping that I would only have one baby this time. I knew I couldn't handle having twins again. I pleaded with God, asking Him to grant me the joy of experiencing the love and care for just one tiny baby at a time. It was a quiet dream of mine, but my fears always seemed to overshadow my desire for a single baby.

As the days went by, my pregnancy progressed, and my emotions were a rollercoaster ride. I found solace in the support of my dad, who always showed me love and understanding. However, the absence of a loving bond with my mother weighed heavily on my heart. I yearned for a genuine connection, for her to accept me and embrace our mother-daughter relationship.

But as I tried to express my feelings to her, hoping for a breakthrough, she simply dismissed my words with indifference. It was as if she couldn't comprehend the pain she caused me, or perhaps she chose not to acknowledge it. Her dismissive attitude only fueled my frustration and deepened the rift between us.

I longed for her to see me for who I truly was—a daughter seeking her mother's love and affection. Yet, every attempt I made to bridge the gap resulted in disappointment. I reached a breaking point and decided to withdraw, choosing not to engage in conversations that only brought me pain.

Despite the challenges, I found peace in knowing that my baby, a precious life growing within me, would bring joy and love into our family. My focus shifted to nurturing myself and the new life I carried, finding strength in the support of my father, and the hope for a brighter future.

The journey ahead was uncertain, with the world grappling with the effects of the ongoing pandemic. Yet, amidst the chaos and uncertainty, I held onto the belief that love would prevail and that the bond between a mother and her child would be a source of unconditional love and healing.

As the days passed, tension grew between my mother and me. It became unbearable to seek her approval and attention constantly. I had reached a breaking point where I decided enough was enough. I refused to play into her manipulative games any longer.

One day, my mother stormed out of the house, leaving us all worried about her well-being. My father urged me to go after her, but I stood my ground. I was tired of constantly chasing after her, seeking validation that I would never receive. I knew deep down that she would come back on her own accord.

After three long hours, my mother finally returned. The silence that had enveloped our relationship for so long was deafening. But this time, I refused to engage in her toxic dynamics. I had made a decision to break free from her manipulation and regain control over my own life.

As the summer came to an end and my parents prepared to fly back home, I reflected on the time we had spent together. It was a difficult journey filled with emotional ups and downs. But during this chaos, I found a newfound strength within myself. I realized that I no longer needed my mother's validation to feel worthy or loved.

With a heavy heart, I bid farewell to my parents at the airport, knowing that things might never be the same again. But I also felt a sense of relief, knowing that I had taken a stand for myself and chosen my own happiness over the constant need for approval.

As I watched their plane disappear into the sky, I held onto the hope that one day, my mother would recognize the impact her behavior had on our relationship. Until then, I knew I had to focus on healing and building a life filled with love and self-acceptance.

One evening, as I rested on the couch after a long day taking care of our twins, my husband arrived home from work. I was already five months pregnant, and I could feel the weight of my growing belly. Instead of offering support or words of encouragement, my husband made a hurtful comment. He remarked that I was getting "too big" and that he didn't find me attractive anymore.

He suggested that I start working out, emphasizing that being pregnant shouldn't stop me from exercising. His words stung, as I was already dealing with insecurities about my changing body. Instead of finding comfort and understanding in my partner, I felt criticized and devalued.

As the weeks went by, my belly grew bigger and my body felt heavier. The doctor's orders to stay off my feet became more crucial with each passing day. My husband, however, couldn't seem to understand or support my need to rest. He would often complain about my lack of physical activity and compare me to women in different countries who continued to work strenuously while pregnant.

But I had learned my lesson from my previous experience with a premature birth, and I was determined not to go through that again. When I reached 28 weeks, my doctor emphasized the importance of minimizing physical exertion to ensure a healthy, full-term pregnancy. I knew I had to prioritize the well-being of my baby over my husband's demands.

Despite his grumbles and disapproval, I made the decision to follow my doctor's advice and stay off my feet as much as possible. I couldn't allow my husband's lack of understanding and support to jeopardize the health and safety of our unborn child. My focus was solely on nurturing and protecting my baby, even if it meant enduring my husband's complaints.

Throughout those challenging weeks, I found solace in the knowledge that I was doing what was best for my child. My love for my baby gave me the strength and determination to ignore the negativity and push through the discomfort. And as I embraced this maternal instinct, I realized that my baby's well-being was more important than seeking validation or approval from my husband.

I held onto the hope that, in time, my husband would come to understand the sacrifices I was making for our growing family. For now, I remained steadfast in my resolve, knowing that the love and determination I had for my baby would guide me through this challenging journey.

At 37 weeks, during a routine doctor's appointment, my blood pressure was once again elevated. The constant struggle with hypertension throughout my pregnancy had me on edge, but I remained hopeful that everything would turn out fine. However, my doctor had a different plan. Concerned about the well-being of both me and the baby, she decided it was time for an emergency C-section.

The news hit me like a wave of mixed emotions. On one hand, I was relieved that the baby would finally be out of harm's way. But on the other hand, the thought of undergoing such a procedure filled me with anxiety. I knew deep down that it was the best decision for both of us, and I trusted my doctor's expertise.

As I drove myself to the hospital, the weight of the situation began to sink in. I couldn't believe that my husband was more concerned about finishing his meal than being by my side during this crucial moment.

Despite his objections, I knew that a C-section was the safest option for me and my baby. I was also determined to undergo tubal ligation at the same time, as I had made the decision that my family was now complete.

Once I arrived at the hospital, the medical staff quickly prepared me for the procedure. As I lay on the operating table, I couldn't help but feel a mix of anxiety and excitement. The thought of finally meeting my baby boy was overwhelming, and I hoped that everything would go smoothly.

The surgical team worked swiftly and efficiently, ensuring the safety of both me and the baby. Moments later, I heard the sweet cry of my newborn, and tears of joy streamed down my face. The long and challenging journey finally led me to this precious moment – the birth of my baby.

Little did I know that this experience would mark the beginning of a journey filled with ups and downs but also with immeasurable love and joy. The road ahead may be uncertain, but with my baby in my arms, I felt ready to face whatever came my way.

The doctors and nurses worked efficiently, ensuring that both my baby and I were in safe hands. As they performed the c-section, I couldn't help but reflect on the journey I had been through during this pregnancy. From dealing with my mother's hurtful words to the constant criticism from my husband, I had weathered it all. But now, at this moment, I was focused on the well-being of my baby and myself.

After what felt like an eternity, I heard the sound of my baby's first cry. Tears welled up in my eyes as the doctors held him up for me to see. He was perfect, a tiny bundle of joy that made all the hardships I had faced worthwhile.

Though the circumstances were far from ideal, I couldn't help but feel a sense of gratitude. My little one had arrived safe and sound despite the complications that arose during the pregnancy. It was a testament to the strength and resilience within me.

As I held my baby boy in my arms, a wave of love and determination washed over me. I was now a mother of three, and nothing would stop me from giving my children the love and care they deserved. In that moment, I made a promise to myself that I would surround them with a supportive and nurturing environment, one that was free from the negativity and criticism that had plagued me for so long.

The road ahead wouldn't be easy, but I knew that I had the strength and resilience to overcome any obstacles that came my way. With my beautiful baby in my arms, I felt a renewed sense of purpose and a deep sense of love. My journey as a mother had just begun, and I was ready to embrace it with all my heart.

After seeking help for my postpartum depression, I began taking antidepressants, and it made a significant difference in my ability to enjoy motherhood. I no longer had the energy to engage with my husband's nonsensical behavior. Surprisingly, he seemed genuinely excited about our baby, especially since he had the privilege of taking a three-month paid paternity leave from the VA hospital where he worked. He spent the first two months by my side, providing support and care, and saved the remaining month for later. It was a relief to have him there during those early months of parenthood.

As the months went by, my husband started to complain about my weight again, despite my efforts to shed the baby weight by using a spinning bike while our little one napped. It seemed like he couldn't be satisfied. He began pressuring me to start thinking about going back to work. I remembered a time in our marriage when he even suggested that I join the military just for the benefits. I firmly stood my ground, refusing to leave my children for months of training.

In an attempt to appease him, I agreed to take the military entrance test, knowing deep down that I would intentionally fail it. I didn't want to be pushed into a path I didn't desire. When I failed the test, he was disappointed, but inside, I felt a sense of relief. It was a way for him to finally leave me alone about joining the military.

Chapter Nineteen
Breaking Point: Confronting Toxicity And Seeking Liberation

Our relationship soon saw wrecking once again. With three kids to care for and a husband visibly dissatisfied with life, the strain between us grew even stronger. Despite our financial stability, my husband insisted I find employment. Even though he earned a comfortable income in California, he felt ashamed that I wasn't working. The irony was not lost on me - here we were, the envy of our street, with me as a stay-at-home mom, yet he yearned for me to contribute financially, disregarding the pride of providing for his own family.

I confided in him about my desire to travel to Poland alone, hoping to confront my fear of being away from my children. Surprisingly, he understood my need for solitude. Despite feeling terrified, I recognized the importance of this journey for my personal growth. With his support, I embarked on a two-week trip to Poland, leaving him in charge of our children with the help of his mother, who flew in to assist him.

After nearly two years of silence, I mustered the courage to visit my childhood home and see my mother. As I entered, anxiety clenched at my chest, but I managed to utter some word hesitantly, saying, "Hi, Mom." Her response shattered me. Without even looking at me, she muttered a greeting and walked away, devoid of any warmth or interest.

There were no hugs, no questions about how I'd been, no invitation for a comforting cup of tea—just her cold indifference. Returning to my brother's house, tears streamed down my face for the remainder of the day. It wasn't the lack of care that hurt the most, as I had long grown past it. It was the realization that, as a mother myself now, I was not able to understand how a mother could dismiss her own daughter so ruthlessly, driven by her own ego. Despite the pain I endured from our past traumas, she chose to cast me as the villain in her narrative. As for me? I had no clue what I did wrong to her!

Even while still relying on antidepressants, I found peace in a place other than my home: the gym. Returning home, I was frustrated with the overwhelming uncertainty of my life, which pushed me to seek a fresh start.

Enrolling in a small gym, I embarked on a journey of self-discovery. The intensity of the workouts demanded my full attention, leaving little room for my intrusive thoughts. With each session, I felt myself growing stronger not only physically but mentally as well—or so I believed.

One evening, consumed by heartache, I found myself overwhelmed by emotion. The tattoo bearing my mother's name on my left wrist, once a symbol of love and seeking validation, now reminded me of a painful reminder of her indifference. With my children asleep and my husband en route from work, I give in to the darkness within me. Gripping sharp scissors, I set out to erase the name carved deep into my skin. Though I had no intention of ending my life, my mind was determined to find peace in the physical act of covering her name with scars.

In that moment, the thought of removing the tattoo didn't even cross my mind; I just yearned for the pain to cease. With trembling hands, I took the scissors to my wrist, slicing at the inked letters over and over again, the cuts shallow but purposeful. As tears streamed down my face, I found myself lying on the floor, the weight of despair pressing upon me.

It was then that my husband entered the room, his gaze cold and indifferent as he said: "I don't have time for this shit," before retreating downstairs to have the meal I had prepared. His callous words and complete disregard for my well-being cut deep, and I couldn't hold back my tears. I pleaded with a higher power, asking for the strength to escape the toxic grip of this relationship.

The next morning, I awoke with a newfound determination never to harm myself again. I vowed to focus on healing, not just for my own sake but for the sake of my children, too.

Immersing myself in the gym became my daily ritual, and it proved to be the best decision I ever made for my mental well-being. The gym organized a weight loss competition spanning six weeks, and to my surprise, I found myself in first place—or so I thought.

In between the gym sessions, I struck up friendships with a few women who seemed kind, but beneath their smiles lay unhealed wounds and simmering jealousy. They envied my positive outlook despite the challenges, my seemingly loving husband who only put on a facade in public, and the life I led, which was far from perfect yet marked by hope. Shock and joy washed over me when the winner was announced and my name was called. For the first time in my life, I had achieved something meaningful for myself, and it filled me with a sense of accomplishment and joy.

Just when I thought my triumph was secure, my supposed friends approached me with a cruel revelation. They confessed to making a mistake in the competition results, snatching away my victory in a bid to rectify their error. I was stunned, not by the loss itself, but by the betrayal of friendship driven by envy.

There were countless ways to address the situation without tarnishing someone else's joy, yet they chose to undermine my happiness. Feeling deeply hurt, I realized they weren't true friends and decided to distance myself from them. Alone in my car, I let my tears fall without restraint. Despite the setback, I made a firm decision to keep going and promised myself to come back stronger in the next competition.

It was then that I began to turn inward, channeling my energy into self-improvement. I embarked on a journey of personal growth, starting with the simple act of reading five pages a day to sharpen my focus. I also sought help from hypnosis sessions to boost my self-esteem, finding it to be a crucial support as I faced the challenges of my marriage with a spouse who constantly undermined my confidence from the very beginning.

In January 2022, I made a firm decision and confronted my husband, informing him that I intended to return to Florida once our twins completed kindergarten. I was resolute and brimming with confidence, tired of molding my life around his desires in California.

Despite his insistence on his dream job, he remained discontented, finding fault in every aspect of our lives. Determined to reclaim control, I threw myself into intense workouts, pushing my body to its limits in pursuit of a slimmer figure. I shed so much weight that acquaintances struggled to recognize me, yet I still saw myself as overweight in the mirror.

My personal trainer grew concerned, urging me to eat more as I teetered on the brink of an eating disorder. In the depths of my mind, I couldn't shake off my husband's words: *"Nobody will accept you with three kids and overweight."* It was as if I was driven by a desire to prove him wrong, to show that I could be thin and desirable despite the challenges I faced.

Despite my inner hope that my husband would finally validate me after losing weight, his response shattered my expectations. He dismissed my achievement, claiming that anyone could accomplish it without much effort. Reading my first book on manipulation opened my eyes to the harsh reality: ***my husband was the epitome of manipulation.***

I understood that staying confused was detrimental to my well-being. One minute, he'd shower me with love, and the next, he'd lash out with hurtful words. This constant emotional turmoil kept me trapped in a toxic cycle, unable to escape its grip.

The moment arrived to return to Florida, leaving behind our rented house and settling back into our home in Dania Beach. Although apprehensive about the possibility of the house still being haunted, I chose to place my trust in God's plan, believing that this move would mark a fresh start for me and my children.

Upon our return, we had enough financial stability for my husband to take a few months off work and enjoy some comfort. While I stayed committed to my gym routine, our intimacy declined, and I stopped drinking alcohol. These shifts hinted at underlying problems. Eventually, my husband started griping about giving up his dream job for our move, expressing frustration over the lack of similar opportunities in Florida.

Amidst his constant prioritization of money over family, my husband approached me one evening with an abrupt question: "Do you want to have sex?!" Shocked by his reaction, I found the strength to refuse, which only fueled his rage. He hurled insults at me, calling me an ungrateful bitch, then retreated to the couch in anger.

Terrified, I resolved to stand firm against the manipulation and mental abuse that had plagued our marriage for far too long. Summoning all my strength, I made a solemn vow that this toxic cycle would end that very night.

The following day, I moved my mattress to the living room, citing my husband's excessive snoring as the reason. His surprise at my refusal was evident, and out of frustration, he proposed that I go to Poland and take a break. To which I happily replied, "Why not." This was because I understood the necessity of a break, not to mend our relationship but to gather the strength needed to end it.

Chapter Twenty
Forging Ahead: Letting Go Of The Past And Embracing New Beginnings

During my time in Poland, I kept to myself, save for visits from my older brother and the unexpected arrival of my father. Their presence provided a sense of comfort and support during my healing journey.

As the days passed, I found peace in their company and the familiar surroundings of my childhood home. When my father suggested joining me on the return trip, I welcomed the idea wholeheartedly.

Upon my arrival back home, I made a decision that altered the course of my life: I confronted my husband and instructed him to leave, urging him to seek refuge with his mother. Despite his facade of being the perfect husband, I knew deep down that he wouldn't put up a fight. This time, I refused to succumb to false hopes or expectations, determined to reclaim my independence and rebuild my life on my own terms.

This time, I made a vow to PRIORITIZE MYSELF. The very next day, I took the bold step of filing for divorce. When my husband approached me, begging on his knees and feigning tears, I remained resolute. I reminded him of the years of neglect and mistreatment I endured, refusing to allow him or anyone else to treat me that way ever again.

During the asset division, I decided to let go of our shared properties, choosing only the first house we bought together. Additionally, I asked for a share of the stocks to ensure a new beginning for me and my kids.

Despite my initial fears about providing for my family alone, I attempted to obtain my realtor license as a potential means of financial stability. However, despite my efforts, I was unable to pass the licensing exam. Although I couldn't comprehend it at the time, I trusted that everything happened for a reason, believing that a new path was unfolding before me.

If I had passed the test, I would have been thrust into a demanding job, leaving my children to figure out our new life without their father present. I knew that diving into work immediately would have prevented me from fully healing and being there for my kids in this critical transition.

So, I made the difficult decision to prioritize their well-being and chose to homeschool them, ensuring they had the support they needed during this difficult time. I explained to them that their father was living elsewhere because constant fighting between us was unhealthy for everyone.

Surprisingly, they seemed to grasp the situation, and I felt a sense of peace wash over me. Finally, the divorce was finalized, and as the weight of the years of mental abuse lifted off my shoulders, I found myself shedding tears of relief for a solid 20 minutes. With the custody agreement settled at a 50/50 split, I embraced the opportunity to focus on nurturing my children in our new reality, especially considering the challenges posed by our less-than-ideal neighborhood and educational system. As time went by, I noticed my ex-husband's erratic behavior affecting the children, and I couldn't stand it.

One day, my daughter couldn't find him outside while he was walking the dogs with my youngest son. She called me in a panic, and I instructed her to return to his apartment and wait for him there. Immediately after, I messaged him, urging him to leave a note for her in case she woke up before his return.

However, his response was far from understanding. He lashed out at my daughter with anger and frustration, questioning why she was involving him in trouble with me. This frightened my daughter, prompting her to ask me to come and get them. Disturbed by his behavior, I obliged and went to fetch them. To my disbelief, his actions escalated further when he attempted to install a hidden baby camera disguised as a USB charger in my own home.

When I confronted him about the hidden camera, he offered a feeble excuse, claiming he wanted to see if I had divorced him for someone else. I promptly rebuffed his justification, asserting that it was his manipulative and abusive behavior that led to our divorce.

Unbothered, he continued to send me messages, warning me against having other men in the house. I chose to ignore his attempts to provoke me and focused on my own well-being and that of my children.

Taking matters into my own hands, I consulted with a lawyer once again and successfully obtained custody arrangements that favored me, reducing his custody to 20%. Upon being served with the legal papers, his immediate concern was regarding child support payments, confirming that money remained his sole priority.

Despite feeling a sense of relief that my children would primarily be under my care, he persisted in accusing me of toxicity and attempting to sever his role as a father. Recognizing his manipulative tactics, I remained steadfast in my determination to focus on my own healing journey and shield my children from his influence.

On one occasion, he went so far as to compare me to my mother, and a remark made all the more absurd by the fact that he didn't even believe in God, let alone divine judgment. Learning to respond to his provocations with a dismissive "cool story," I dug deeper into my own healing process, recognizing his behavior as a reflection of his own insecurities and weaknesses.

Six months later, despite initial hesitation, I found myself entertaining the idea of having lunch with my ex-husband and our children. Though plagued by doubts and fears of regressing into past patterns of fear and conflict, I ultimately decided to embrace the opportunity as a part of my healing journey.

To my surprise, the encounter left me feeling peaceful and content. As he took the children to the playground afterward, I found myself overwhelmed with emotions, shedding tears of happiness and pride at the progress I had made in overcoming anger and resentment. It was a significant milestone in my journey toward healing and self-discovery.

I came to realize that forgiveness wasn't about giving someone else a chance but about granting myself the peace I so desperately needed. Holding onto anger only tethered me to the past, preventing me from moving forward.

Embracing forgiveness allowed me to let go of that burden and find solace in my heart and mind. It was a transformative realization: *without forgiveness, true peace remained elusive.* Cutting negative influences out of my life became imperative, even if it meant facing solitude.

Surprisingly, I discovered a profound sense of contentment in that newfound aloneness. It was liberating to realize how much I could grow and thrive without the weight of negativity dragging me down. I understood that healing was impossible in an environment that caused me pain. Although it was difficult to comprehend why those I cared about had hurt me, I recognized that their presence in my life had served a purpose— to teach me to love myself, even if they couldn't love me in return.

Chapter Twenty-One
Healing Wounds: Embracing Forgiveness And Inner Strength

As I continued to heal, life threw constant tests my way, tempting me to return to my old habits. I used to drink alcohol, but I quit for good before we returned to Florida. I used to smoke marijuana, but I quit once I returned from Poland. Despite my neighbors smoking every day and offering me some, I stayed strong and declined. I even acknowledged that smoking had masked the red flags in my relationship with my husband.

Once, my ex-husband asked if his new car could be delivered to my house while he was away in California for his military weekend drill. I agreed, promising myself not to stoop to his level, no matter how much he had hurt me. When the car arrived, I was taken aback by his shallowness. He had bought my dream car, BMW Series 7, a car he never wanted or liked.

I sat by the car, pondering his intentions. Did he expect me to be jealous, or did he anticipate me running back to him? Regardless, I reminded myself that my peace of mind was priceless. No amount of material possessions could lure me back to him. Ironically, fate intervened when a flood hit South Florida, destroying his prized car. It served as a stark reminder that buying the car was a misguided decision, and karma had a way of balancing the scales.

The day after the flood, schools were closed due to the water everywhere. Thankfully, my house wasn't flooded, but my shed suffered some damage. As I stood outside on Friday afternoon, around 5 pm, I heard a loud noise and then felt a sharp pain in my leg. I thought a rock had been thrown at me by my friend's kid.

When I looked down, I saw that my leg was bleeding. I tried to move, but there was something strange stuck behind my leg, causing me pain. I decided to leave it alone and went inside to put a band-aid on the wound. However, the pain persisted, so I called my ex-husband to take me to the ER. He was eager to help, perhaps seeing it as an opportunity to reconcile.

My friend stayed with my kids while we rushed to the ER. I explained the situation to the nurses and anyone who came to see me, but they seemed skeptical. I was genuinely clueless about what had happened—I just felt a sharp pain in my leg. They took an x-ray to check for broken bones.

When the person from the x-ray department returned, they started yelling at me, accusing me of lying. I was stunned and asked what they meant. They said there was a bullet in my leg and accused me of making up my story. My jaw dropped—I couldn't believe it. The doctor said we needed to call the police, and I agreed.

As I recounted the events to the detective, my emotions overwhelmed me, and tears streamed down my face. It wasn't because of the pain but because I couldn't shake the thought that my 3-year-old son and my friend's son had been there, too. The idea that it could have been one of them hit me hard. I thanked my lucky stars that it was only me who got hurt. I realized at that moment that I would do anything to protect my children, even take a bullet for them.

The nurse removed the bullet—it was 45 mm, which seemed huge to me. Thankfully, it had missed my bone and only grazed my muscle. They sent me home with antibiotics. Despite my fears, I knew I had to be strong for my kids and face my fears head-on, setting an example for them.

With trembling hands and a heart heavy with anxiety, I ventured outside and settled onto a bench. I knew I had to face my fears head-on; running away would only give them power over me. My ex-husband suggested I move out and find a new place, but I refused. I couldn't let fear dictate my life. Instead, I chose to see the blessing in being alive. I channeled my fear into positive energy, reminding myself that things could have been much worse—I could have lost my life or my child.

Despite my efforts, complications arose. An infection took hold inside my leg, but I remained vigilant, taking antibiotics and undergoing weeks of treatment. Finally, after three weeks of struggling to heal the infection on my own, I was admitted to the hospital for surgery.

As they sliced through my flesh, removing part of my muscle, I lay in the hospital bed for four agonizing nights. Every three hours, the sharp prick of the IV pierced my veins, delivering potent antibiotics that felt like fire coursing through my body. Alone and in pain, I found solace in prayer, pleading with God for the strength to endure not the physical agony but the overwhelming loneliness. There were moments when the emptiness seemed unbearable when I longed so desperately for human connection that even the thought of embracing my ex-husband crossed my mind.

But I held firm, reminding myself that quenching my thirst with poison would only lead to further suffering. I kept my ordeal hidden from my children, shielding them from the trauma of my struggle. Unable to return to the gym, my sanctuary, for six long weeks, I faced a crucial test. Would I succumb to despair and revert to my old self, or would I cling to the belief that everything happens for a reason? With every ounce of determination, I fought to preserve my faith, refusing to let this trial break me.

Two months later, craving to heal my wounded inner child, I whisked my kids away to Poland for a rejuvenating summer retreat. We settled into a cozy house by the tranquil lake where I had cherished memories of my childhood. Determined to create a nurturing environment, I opted not to stay with my parents, knowing their presence wouldn't foster the healing we needed.

Despite the pain and resentment I harbored toward my mother, I chose to be the epitome of kindness and compassion. Deep within, I forgave her, though she remained unaware, likely to misconstrue my gesture as her own need for forgiveness. My intention wasn't to prove my superiority but to offer her the kindness she so desperately craved, knowing that her wounds ran deep and required gentleness to mend.

As I sat there, surrounded by the echoes of my past, I marveled at the peace that enveloped me. No longer did my mother's presence trigger the familiar pains of yesteryears. Instead, I remained serene, untouched by the ghosts of my past. It was a moment of profound pride as I realized the extent of my healing journey.

Every trial and tribulation I endured had led me to this moment of unshakeable tranquility. Through the depths of my pain, I discovered the true meaning of compassion, learning to extend it unconditionally to others and to withhold judgment.

In that moment, I felt richer than any material wealth could offer. The peace I had found was priceless, a treasure born from the depths of my own struggles.

Chapter Twenty-Two
A Journey Of Healing: From Pain To Peace

While in Poland, I found myself surrounded by familiar faces that once stirred painful emotions within me. But this time, something had changed. I had undergone a profound healing, and it transformed the way I interacted with these individuals.

Instead of allowing their presence to reignite old wounds, I approached them with kindness and compassion. I understood that they, too, carried their own burdens and struggles, just as I had. This shift in perspective allowed me to extend empathy where there was once resentment, and it brought a sense of deep fulfillment and peace to my soul.

As the evening unfolded, my brother, sister, their spouses, and my mother gathered together, indulging in drinks and laughter. Despite the familial atmosphere, I felt out of place amidst the revelry. Sensing that this wasn't my scene, I quietly excused myself and retreated to bed early, seeking peace of mind in the company of my children.

In the stillness of the night, disturbed by distant echoes of heated voices, I stirred from my slumber. Peering through the glass patio door, I witnessed the scene unfold: my family, consumed by alcohol-fueled arguments, their voices rising in discord.

Although intrigued, I remained seated, wary of being drawn into their heated conversation. As the night wore on, my brother's words cut through the tension, revealing his deep-seated pain and unresolved childhood wounds. His anguish mirrored my own, echoing sentiments I had long suppressed. Yet, amidst the turmoil, I realized that our mother remained steadfast in her denial, deflecting blame onto others.

It was clear to me that she would never admit to her mistakes. My brother hoped she would, but I knew better. I accepted her for who she was and it helped me cope with life. I learned not to expect people to change if they don't want to.

It all started when my brother and I caught our mother cheating when we were teenagers. We found messages about her having an affair with a man who was staying at our hotel. It was a painful discovery.

When we confronted her, she lashed out at my brother, blaming him and me for all the fights in the house. She accused us of lying to Dad about her cheating. It was a heavy burden for us to bear at such a young age.

In a burst of frustration, my brother's voice pierced the tense air, his words a sharp rebuke against our mother's denials. He demanded the truth, unwilling to tolerate any more deception. Our mother's feeble defense crumbled under the weight of his accusation, her admission revealing a profound loneliness masked by her actions. With heavy hearts, we listened as my sister voiced our collective disappointment, highlighting the stark contrast between a mother's duty to nurture and her selfish actions.

As I sat there, the pain in my siblings' voices cut through the room, each word heavy with the weight of unhealed wounds. Their anguish echoed my own struggles, a shared journey of suffering and resilience. In that moment, I offered a silent prayer for their healing, wishing for them the same solace I sought for myself. I understood their turmoil intimately, having walked alongside them through life's trials and tribulations.

Despite the raw emotions surfacing, I refrained from passing judgment, recognizing the complexities of their experiences. It was a poignant reminder of the importance of empathy and understanding, a testament to the unseen battles each person faces.

I always share with my children a valuable lesson: treat others as you would want to be treated. When someone isn't kind to you, that's when it's most important to show them kindness. As I guide my children through life, I emphasize the importance of staying true to themselves, even if others try to pressure them into doing otherwise.

A true friend, whether it's a friend, partner, or parent, will never pressure you into doing something that makes you uncomfortable. Facing our fears is different—it's a natural part of life. We're born with just two fears: the fear of falling and the fear of sudden loud noises. All other fears develop as we grow and experience life.

When we look at children, we often marvel at their carefree nature. That's because, at birth, we're only equipped with two primary emotions: peace and love. However, as we journey through life, we learn and experience a wide range of emotions. While emotions can be powerful tools, I've learned that it's important not to dwell on the negative ones for too long.

Embracing the power of positivity was a crucial part of my healing journey. Whenever negativity crept in, I made a conscious effort to counter it with three positive thoughts. I discovered that the more positive energy I radiated, the more positivity I attracted into my life. It was like a magnetic force, drawing in goodness and repelling negativity.

During my healing process, I realized a profound truth: *we often attract people who mirror our own state of being.* If I was unhealed, I found myself entangled with partners who were also grappling with their own wounds. It was a harsh reality to confront, but it underscored the importance of prioritizing my own healing journey.

Putting myself first and committing to self-healing became my top priorities. I understood that healing wasn't just about overcoming past traumas—it was also a crucial step toward achieving success and fulfillment in life. It required belief in oneself and a willingness to invest time and effort into personal growth.

The greatest gift you can give yourself is unwavering faith in your own abilities. It doesn't matter if others doubt you; what truly matters is your belief in yourself.

As humans, we often find ourselves caught between dwelling on the past and worrying about the future. I know this struggle all too well, having battled depression and anxiety myself.

In the past, I was consumed by regret and sorrow, constantly replaying old memories in my mind. At the same time, I fretted endlessly about what the future held, fearing the unknown and questioning every decision I made.

But then, I discovered the power of living in the present moment. By letting go of my fixation on the past and my anxieties about the future, I found peace and contentment in the here and now.

I learned to trust in the unfolding of life's journey, embracing the unknown with open arms. And you know what? It brought me the greatest joy and fulfillment I've ever known.

So, if you're struggling with similar feelings, I urge you to take a moment to breathe and focus on the present. Trust that the universe has a plan for you, and believe that it will lead you to the life you've always dreamed of.

The more gratitude I cultivated in my life, the more blessings seemed to flow my way. Every morning, I made it a ritual to wake up and count ten things I was grateful for, allowing that gratitude to infuse my day with positive energy.

I came to understand that gratitude isn't just a feeling; it's a powerful force that attracts abundance into our lives. It helps us appreciate the present moment and find joy in even the smallest blessings.

As humans, it's natural to desire more than what we have, but true fulfillment comes when we're grateful for what we already possess.

I remember when I lived in a small house, I cherished it deeply, recognizing it as a place of warmth and shelter. And when the opportunity arose to move into a larger home with a pool, I embraced it with gratitude, never forgetting the humble beginnings that shaped my journey.

Through it all, I've learned to never take my life experiences for granted. There are always others who would give anything to walk in our shoes, reminding us to appreciate the beauty of our own unique journey.

When I was struck by a bullet, I didn't dwell on the question, "Why me?" Instead, I found solace in the fact that I was still breathing, grateful that it hadn't been my children in harm's way.

Reflecting on my journey, I realized that every trial and tribulation has molded me into the person I am today. Despite the hardships, I wouldn't hesitate to endure them all over again if it meant arriving at this moment of peace and self-love.

Today, I stand as a living testament to the power of resilience and inner strength. I am filled with pride for the person I've become – someone who exudes peace, love, and kindness in every aspect of life.

Through my story, I aim to inspire others to believe in the possibility of a happy ending. Not the kind bought with money or material possessions, but the genuine, heartfelt joy of living a life filled with peace and contentment.

We often witness individuals who possess immense wealth yet remain trapped in the clutches of unhappiness. It's a stark reminder that true peace and love are invaluable treasures that cannot be bought with riches alone.

Embarking on a journey of self-discovery requires immense courage, bravery, and, above all, love for oneself. Though the path may be fraught with challenges and tears, I assure you, ***every step is worth it.***

It's crucial not to lose sight of our own worth along the way. Transformation doesn't happen overnight, but with perseverance and unwavering belief in ourselves, we can achieve the life we've always dreamed of.

Remember, the key lies in embracing our own potential and the boundless possibilities that await when we trust in ourselves and the vision we hold for our lives.

As I close this chapter of my life's journey, I do so with a heart brimming with gratitude and hope. Despite the trials and tribulations, I stand tall, knowing that every obstacle I've overcome has brought me closer to the person I am today.

I am filled with an overwhelming sense of peace and contentment, knowing that I have emerged from the darkness into the warm embrace of light and love. And as I look ahead to the chapters of my life yet to unfold, I do so with a renewed sense of purpose and excitement.

For I know that the best is yet to come, and with each passing day, I move closer to the life I've always dreamed of—a life filled with boundless joy, love, and endless possibilities. So, here's to new beginnings, to embracing the journey, and to never giving up on the beautiful story that is our own.